MAKING TIME

MAKING TIME

GERARD HARGREAVES
DOROTHY MORFETT
GERALDINE BOWN

BBC Books

This book is published to accompany the
television series entitled *Making Time*
which was first broadcast in March 1993
Published by BBC Books,
a division of BBC Enterprises Limited,
Woodlands, 80 Wood Lane
London W12 0TT

First published 1993
ISBN 0 563 36932 9

Designed by Chris Bell
Set in Palatino by Ace Filmsetting Ltd, Frome
Printed and bound in Great Britain by
BPCC Hazells Ltd
Member of BPCC Ltd

Cover printed by Clays Ltd, St Ives Plc

A time management training video, based on the BBC series is
available from BBC Training Videos, tel: 081-576 2361

CONTENTS

INTRODUCTION

Making Time is the book for anyone who is having trouble juggling the various calls on their time – work, children, running a home and the other hundred and one tasks that have to be fitted into a day.

The book is divided into three sections. Part one, written by Gerard Hargreaves, deals with managing your time at work. It shows you how to devise a work pattern to suit you, how to delegate, how to cope with meetings and endless interruptions, and how to set goals. Part two, written by Dorothy Morfett, discusses working at home, including essential advice for people running a business from their home. For people searching for a job, there are helpful guidelines showing how to make the most of your time and resources. Part three of this book, written by Geraldine Bown, shows how to juggle your various responsibilities as a working parent and still have time for yourself.

The text is divided up with quizzes and checklists so you can chart your progress from leading a disorganized, chaotic life to achieving that perfect balance of work, rest and play.

PART ONE

MANAGING YOUR TIME IN THE OFFICE

T HE first part of this book deals with managing your time in the office. There are two components of good time management:

- The impact of your working pattern on your time management,
- Tips and effective working practices for good time management.

They are both crucial if you are serious about developing the way you manage your time. Think of it as an expensive sports car – if you look inside the car it will have all the latest electric gadgets, an amazing sound system and the finest quality leather upholstery. All good-looking, but if the engine is not running properly the car is pretty useless in terms of achieving its purpose – to get you from A to B.

The same is true for time management. We all know people who have the latest time management gadgets; the leather diary system, electronic organizers, wall charts etc, but they are still late for meetings, miss deadlines and have to work late. Why? Because the engine that is driving the gadgets is not running smoothly. The engine in this case is themselves!

The first part of this section deals with tuning the engine and developing your own working pattern. Once you have an effective pattern you will find it easier to take on board the tips and working practice. Although this section focuses on the office, many of the ideas and suggestions can equally be applied in your non-working lives, and some of these ideas will be developed later in the back of the book.

As you go through this section, make a note of the action points you intend to try. At the end of this part there is a place for you to record the key action points that you are really going to try and make work. Once you have written them, make a note in your diary in two months' time to check them. If you are doing most of them it should be making a major impact on your time management. Good luck!

CHAPTER ONE

TIME MANAGEMENT AND YOU

T HE way you manage your time is very much a reflection of your own personality. Your personality will help to determine your working pattern which in turn will to some extent determine the way you manage your time. If you want to change the way you manage your time you may have to change your work patterns.

WORK PATTERNS

Thirty years ago American cardiologists Meyer Friedman and Ray Rosenman explored the connection between work patterns and heart disease. They discovered two distinct styles or patterns which they called Type A and Type B. How can these patterns be identified? Watch people as they go about their work and see if you can recognize these characteristics.

Type A	Type B
Sense of urgency	Relaxed
Competitive	Takes time to make decision
Walks/moves quickly	Walks slower
Eats quickly	Thoughtful
Hates delay	Good listener
Feels guilty when relaxing	Lots of relaxing hobbies
Impatient	Patient

Our individual style has a powerful effect on how we behave and on our whole approach to time management. These two case studies should help clarify these patterns. As you read them think about yourself and your colleagues and see if any bells ring!

A DAY IN THE LIFE OF ...

ROGER 'A' FIELDING

Roger is up and out of the house in fifteen or twenty minutes depending on whether or not he can find an ironed shirt. Breakfast is snatched from the toaster on his way out the door. He hates hanging around when there is work to be done. As nobody else is yet in the office, Roger makes a coffee and goes through the unsorted mail. He opens, reads and leaves his mail in the in-tray for further action. He only does the really quick and easy things immediately as he must get on.

It is relatively quiet in the office so he does about half an hour of uninterrupted work on the presentation he has to give at 10.30 a.m. Unfortunately just as he is about to do a quick rehearsal, the phone rings and he is distracted. In fact this phone call marks the start of the daily routine of interruptions: easy problems get quick answers, more difficult ones get put off with promises of further investigation and action. Roger prides himself on never having to say no. However, he does recognize that as his focus tends to switch rapidly between different areas, his concentration levels remain relatively low.

Roger has to run to make his 10.30 meeting and is glad one or two people arrive later than him. His presentation goes well – though it would have been nice to have had an overhead projector – but, as always, his confidence and energy win the day. Although everyone else is most impressed, Roger secretly worries that one of these days he will fail to snatch success from the jaws of disaster.

Roger would like to get out for lunch but rarely finds the time. Today is no exception.

Back in the office he receives a phone call from his boss. She reminds him of a report she delegated to him and requests an update at 2 p.m. He had completely forgotten about it and works through lunch in order to cover his embarrassment.

Roger manages to bluff his way through the meeting with a promise of more work on the report over the weekend. Again he returns to his office. By now his in-tray is so full that even he realizes he is not going to be able to get through all his work that day.

He decides to delegate the more urgent pieces to his team. He feels quite happy doing this as people always say he should delegate more. But two of his subordinates are a little upset: they have booked a squash court for 5.30 p.m. and will now have to cancel. The mutiny is quickly crushed with a reminder of the unemployment figures and the fact that he himself rarely gets away from the office before 7 p.m. Roger takes no nonsense from his team!

The rest of the afternoon flies by in a whirlwind of activity and it is only after everyone has gone home that Roger again manages to get on with some uninterrupted work. Unfortunately he is unable to advance the most important thing in his tray which requires some information from a client. He missed them when he phoned at 5.45 p.m. Nevertheless, there are hundreds of other things to keep him busy until 7.30 p.m. when suddenly he realizes it is his wedding anniversary and he's late.

At that precise second the phone rings. It is his wife!

> 'Roger darling, I'm afraid I'm still at the office sorting a few things out ...'

Once again Roger's luck had held!

A DAY IN THE LIFE OF ...

HARRY 'B' HODGSON

In contrast to Roger, Harry's start to the day is very much more leisurely. He helps get the children up and takes time to sit down for breakfast with his family. Harry likes to take his time and enjoy life.

He allows plenty of time to get to the office. He has invested in a good car radio and sees the slow drive to work as time well spent keeping abreast with world events by listening to the news.

On arrival in the office Harry spends some time chatting to other members of his team under the guise of a daily briefing. While he is happy giving general direction, he rarely makes decisions without a lot of deliberation. This means these meetings take far longer than necessary and end without clear action points for participants.

Once Harry gets into his office he is difficult to dislodge. His powers of concentration are impressive and his eye for detail sometimes borders on the fanatical. It has become a standing joke that he rarely approves any work until it has been drafted five times.

This morning Harry has to present to the Board at 10.30 a.m. and is not at all confident. He has set aside an hour to go through his material and do final checks. He is still not entirely happy with the script and makes one or two changes even at this late stage. He goes down to the room about 15 minutes early just to run through his material one final time using the slide projector.

Harry's slot is just after his colleague Roger Fielding, whose presentations always make him feel thoroughly inadequate. Having seen him present without visual aids and apparently without notes Harry is tempted to try the same. Fortunately he resists! Everyone seems quite impressed, though he would have liked them to be a little more enthusiastic – perhaps they failed to grasp the finer points of his argument.

Harry does not go back to the office but goes out for lunch with a client. He enjoys doing business over lunch. He feels it is important to know his clients and believes firmly that they use him because they like him. He works hard to be the friendly face of commerce.

On returning to the office, Harry finds a note from his boss reminding him that he has been asked for estimates of next year's expenses by 3 p.m. Harry has already worked out some preliminary figures but is unsure how to present them and anyway is worried about all the variables that could affect them. He decides to go up and see his boss to talk them through. Unfortunately his boss is rather busy so Harry finds his figures dismissed as far too complicated: 'I'll put you down for the same as all the other teams in your area, OK?'

As he walks back to his office, Harry passes two of Roger's team in the corridor. They are clearly upset about something and, as Harry is well known as a good listener, they pour out their grievances to him. Harry sympathizes, without being disloyal to Roger. Although he does not say it, he cannot understand how anyone can be so hard-nosed with his staff.

Ironically when Harry gets back to his office, he finds a document he has delegated back in his in-tray. As he looks through it he feels that as usual he does not seem to have put across what he wanted accurately enough and as a result finds himself 'polishing' to a point where the original is almost obliterated by amendments. By the time he finishes he just misses the last post and has to send the document to its destination by courier.

Harry's in-tray is full of small bits and pieces that have been collecting throughout the day, in particular a number of trivial issues needing fast decisions. However, it is 5.30 p.m. so Harry tidies his desk and leaves. He likes to be home before the children have gone to bed.

As he drives home Harry reflects that he is unlikely to get to the top of the corporate tree. But what good is success of this type if you are too busy to enjoy its fruits?

I'm sure we can all recognize some Type A people and some Type B people in our office. One is not better than the other, they just have different styles of working. Both have their good and bad points when it comes to time management. Most of us have some Type A and some Type B characteristics in our work pattern. The following exercise should help you identify your own pattern.

WORK PATTERNS EXERCISE –
ASSESSING YOURSELF

For each of the following qualities there are two statements. If you think the left-hand statement best reflects you, circle 1. If the right-hand statement is you, then circle 5. Shades of in-between are represented by 2, 3 and 4, depending on which you feel closest to. Try to avoid too many 3s!

1	A bit last minute, often rushed and late	1 2 3 4 5	Very punctual, never late
2	Very competitive	1 2 3 4 5	Relaxed, not too competitive
3	Tend to interrupt, when others are talking	1 2 3 4 5	Allow others time to finish what they are saying
4	Try to do many things at once; always thinking of next steps	1 2 3 4 5	Take one thing at at a time
5	Quick and loud in speech, may bang and shout	1 2 3 4 5	Slow, deliberate talker
6	Fast mover, walking, eating, driving, etc	1 2 3 4 5	Slow deliberate mover
7	Hide emotions and feelings; they can be a sign of weaknesses	1 2 3 4 5	Happy to express emotions and feelings; we are all human
8	Few interests outside work; do not have time for them	1 2 3 4 5	Wide range of interests and social life
9	Ambitious and eager for promotion	1 2 3 4 5	Enjoy the present; take life as it comes
10	Feeling good about myself is important – forget what others say	1 2 3 4 5	Like to feel part of teams – other people are important

SCORING

When you have finished the exercise add up the circles and divide by 10.

1–2 Strong Type A
2–3 Type A tendencies
3–4 Type B tendencies
4–5 Strong Type B

Whilst this is not aimed at any in-depth analysis it should help to identify your strengths and weaknesses and the areas where you need to take action. Few people are exclusively Type A or Type B. Most of us are a mixture of the two but generally have a leaning one way or the other.

POTENTIAL PROBLEM AREAS FOR TYPES A AND B

Type A

Work Control
Take on work without thinking through consequences – time, people, budget, etc.

Delegation
Tend to hover.

Planning
Great long-term visionaries but tend to lack detailed planning, easily get bored with this.

People
Do not have much time for others, can be abrasive and aggressive; not always good team members.

Relaxing
Rarely relax – often feel guilty. Hobbies tend to be fast and aggressive, few team games.

Priorities
Everything tends to be high priority. Tend to butterfly through the day ending up with lots of tasks partly done, and very few completed.

Type B

Goals
Often lack clear goals in work, career and life in general.

Delegation
Find letting go difficult or give vague instructions.

People
Although generally good with people, find difficulty saying no and confronting people. Try to avoid conflict.

Quality
Very thorough but can go overboard sometimes. Can give a £5,000 answer to a £1,000 question.

Many of the characteristics in our work patterns are good and are the reasons why we were chosen to do the job we do. However, there are some which hinder our performance which we should identify and work on.

ACTION POINTS FOR TYPE A BEHAVIOUR

In work terms your eyes are bigger than your stomach! As a result you may have one of two tendencies: either you will take bites out of a number of pieces of work and never finish any of them, or you will end up with chronic indigestion!

Here are some tips which may help you curb some of the excesses of your Type A behaviour:

- **Take a step back** – look at the balance between work, family and you (hobbies, relaxation, health). Have you got the right balance? Start to take steps to make that balance.
- **Set attainable goals** – be realistic about what you can achieve. This should be done with the help of your boss and colleagues at work and your partner and family at home.
- **Plan how to achieve your goals** – once set, take time out to plan how you are going to meet your goals, then set a time to evaluate them, perhaps 3 months ahead.
- **Delegate** – decide what you can realistically do and what you should pass to others.
- **Aim to relax more** – pay more attention to your health and stress levels. You may try to become physically fitter, plan to leave work earlier, leave work in the office and share more time with your family and friends. Do not feel guilty – you do not have to keep on proving how good or effective you are.
- **Make time for people** – by blocking out time in your diary for talking to staff and building relationships.
- **Say no** – do not over-commit yourself. Never take on a task without asking yourself if you have the time, resources, people, budget, etc. It is better to say no early on than saying yes and not delivering the goods.

ACTION POINTS FOR TYPE B BEHAVIOUR

You are in danger of making the best enemy of the good, of allowing quality to get in the way of genuine achievement.

Here are some tips which may help you curb some of the excesses of your Type B behaviour:

- **Set quantitative goals** – make sure quantity as well as quality feature in your goals. Start to measure your performance by figures and firm up on some of your more abstract ideas.
- **Stop procrastinating** – do it now! Avoid putting off things, you will only have to come back to them later, by which time they will probably be more pressing or difficult.
- **Become more assertive** – do not be afraid to express your feelings and opinions.
- **Assess appropriate level of quality** – beware of trying to do everything to perfection. Cultivate the knack of assessing what is an appropriate standard.

ACTION PLANS

Having examined your own work patterns, list the actions you need to take to make your working pattern more effective. Remember that most of us are a mixture of A and B so you may have actions from both patterns.

What was the score from your Work Patterns Exercise?

SCORE ....   Type A or B..............................

Action Plan

Action Plan

Action Plan

PROCRASTINATION

Procrastination is the art of convincing yourself that you can put off until tomorrow what you should be doing today. It is quite rightly called the 'thief of time' and can hinder our productivity.

Procrastination affects both Type A and Type B people although usually in different ways. Type A people usually leave things until the last minute. They convince themselves that they thrive on the adrenaline induced by the deadline. This has little regard for the chaos it creates for other people or for the effect of a last minute hitch. Type B will often start something but get so bogged down in the planning and preparation stage that they get bored before they begin the main part. They usually end up collecting so much data and information that they lose sight of the end product or find something that really excites them and end up going off on a tangent. They may become the world's expert on minutia X at the expense of completing the main task.

WHY DO WE PROCRASTINATE?

We all have tasks we would rather not do. These generally fall under two headings:
- Boredom, e.g. standard returns in triplicate,
- Fear, e.g. presenting a proposal to your boss.

AREAS OF PROCRASTINATION

Just as every individual has different likes and dislikes, so we all have different areas of procrastination. Here are some of the most common areas in which people put off doing things they should:

Difficult people
Difficult phone calls
Public contacts
Boring tasks
Large projects
Small tasks
Risky/unfamiliar work

Pick the two which you find are a particular problem and make them the focus of your attention over the next few weeks.

HOW DO WE PROCRASTINATE?

We all have our different ways!
- **Small versus large** – we often busy ourselves with the simple, easy and quick tasks leaving the large ones until later, but later never comes!
- **Perfectionist** – we tell ourselves because we haven't got the right information or all the facts or figures we can't begin. Often this is just an excuse to delay starting something.

- **Phoning at lunch** – we often make those difficult calls at lunchtime or late in the day. That way we avoid speaking directly to the person and leave a message. The sticky note goes on their phone, our conscience is clear and the problem has gone away ... until they phone back!
- **'Waste of time'** – we convince ourselves that some tasks, especially small ones, are unnecessary. What might seem small and unnecessary to you could be important for somebody else. They could be waiting for the information to enable them to progress their job.
- **Avoiding the task** – when we are faced with a task we would rather not do we may go for a wander round, make another cup of coffee or allow ourselves to get dragged into other people's conversations. Many people spend longer on the telephone or hang around at the end of meetings because they cannot face that task. All of this might be fun at the time but it does not help us progress our work.

Having identified the areas of our job where we procrastinate and the ways we do it, we must now work to overcome it. The next time you come across one of the tasks apply some time management principles to help you get started. Remember *do it now* or you will only have to come back to it later!

ACTION PLAN FOR LESS PROCRASTINATION

- **Commit yourself to start times** – whenever you are faced with a deadline do not think when you should finish it but when you should start it. The start time should go into the diary more so than the deadline. If you get the start time right, the deadline should follow as a matter of course.
- **Break large projects down into manageable portions** – when faced with a large daunting task spend a few minutes planning how you are going to approach it. Give each phase a start time and tick each one off when you complete it. This will give you a sense of achievement as the task progresses, rather than waiting until the end.
- **Control the amount of paper on your desk** – the more paper you have on your desk the easier you will become distracted. The moment you are faced with an unpleasant task or

become bored your eyes will wander and find something easier or more exciting. You will go off at a tangent and never complete that task. If you are not going to deal with a piece of paper that day, file it and have a bring-forward system in your diary. You can buy concertina files with a space for each day of the month. Put the work in the day you plan to deal with it, take it out that day and action it.

● **Prioritize your tasks** – a 'to do' list without some kind of priority next to each task is asking for trouble. You will tend to chose the easy tasks or the ones you enjoy doing and leave the others until later. It might be that the others are higher priority and should be started first.

A 'to do' list which is nothing more than a memory jogger is limited in it usefulness. An effective 'to do' list should look something like this.

Item to do	Priority	Start Date	End Date	Delegate to	Review	Done

This turns the shopping list into a useful exercise in good time management.

● **Reward yourself** – give yourself a deadline and then plan a treat when you reach it. This will give you something to look forward to.

CHAPTER TWO

TIME MANAGEMENT AND OTHERS

T HE previous chapter concentrated on your own impact on your time management. Very few of us work in isolation from others. Other people's time management has an impact on us just as our time management influences them. You may be the most amazing manager of time but if your boss, peers or those working for you are bad managers of time, it will effect you.

Two important areas of our work that involve interacting with others are:
● Delegated work
● Attending meetings

How many times have we delegated work and it has not been done or not come back quite right. This usually involves us in a last minute rush to correct the job to meet the deadline. Conversely, how often have we been given a task by our boss and not really had a clue what we are supposed to do. We then spend ages working out what we think is required and get it wrong! This is dumping rather than delegating – we all know a lot of people who are good at this! Effective delegation can save time and improve the morale of all concerned.

Most of us spend a percentage of our working day in meetings. Some of us chair meetings, some attend as participants. Whatever capacity you attend the meeting in, you have a role in helping that meeting to be a success and a good use of time. There is often opportunity to manage meetings slightly differently so that they achieve more in less time.

DELEGATION

Whether we are a delegator or a delegatee, the ability to get things done through effective delegation is the cornerstone of good self-management. Understanding a few basic concepts makes it easier.

WHY DELEGATE?

- To give you more time to concentrate on priority work.
- To develop and motivate your people.
- To make use of other people's specialist skills.
- To ensure an even spread of work across the team.
- To do things quicker by concurrent activity.

WHY PEOPLE DON'T DELEGATE

- Unable or unwilling to let go.
- Lack of faith in subordinates' abilities.
- Fear that the subordinates will perform better.
- Believing you can do it quicker and better yourself.
- Like to give impression of being overworked.
- Enjoying doing the job – 'getting their hands dirty'.
- Lack of training.
- Difficult or aggressive subordinates.
- No time to work out what the job entails.

WHAT TO DELEGATE

- Routine jobs, together with attendant responsibility and power to make decisions.
- Whole jobs – to give a sense of achievement.
- Jobs that others can do better and probably more cheaply too.
  Remember delegation is not simply downwards. It maybe sideways or even upwards. You can also delegate to your computer if you take time to learn its various functions.

WHAT NOT TO DELEGATE

- Accountability for the task – it is part of your job that you are delegating.

- New tasks without guidance or training.
- Unpleasant tasks which are really your responsibility.

ACTIONS FOR EFFECTIVE DELEGATION

- **Delegate early** – when possible plan your delegation well in advance and delegate early. Plan the key dates, resources, people you need and necessary training. If your boss is not a planner, then the emphasis rests with you. Plan ahead yourself and suggest you make a start early.
- **Give a clear brief and gain agreement** – ensure all concerned understand exactly what is expected. Brief them clearly on:
    objectives – what exactly is required
    resources – people, money, materials
    priority – be clear on dates and priorities
  Be prepared to invest time in the early stages to explain, demonstrate and coach – it will pay off in the end.
- **Agree review dates and stick to them** – with longer term delegation it is essential to note review dates in your diary. Once delegated it is easy to forget about the task until it is too late. If you agree what is to be achieved by each review you will have an excellent opportunity to:
    – pool the best of new ideas and approaches
    – give praise and recognition
    – maintain focus on the job
- **Establish a 'last time'** – agree a 'last time' date which allows a buffer time to the official deadline. This will ensure there is time to re-do anything that is wrong.
- **Delegate whole jobs** – this not only gives a sense of achievement, it develops others and frees up more of your time.
- **Don't hover** – be available for help when needed, but do not hover. If you have ever worked for a hoverer you know how annoying it can be. Review meetings should reduce the need to hover.
- **On completion** – accept what is good enough, do not 'nit pick'. Accept that the task may have been done differently to how you may have done it. Praise in public, criticize in private.

MEETINGS

For many people meetings have a major impact on their time management. They can be very costly both in terms of money and time. A successful meeting is time and money well spent. A meeting which fails to achieve its aims is a waste of time and money.

TYPES OF MEETINGS

Meetings can be classed under the following headings:
- **Formal** – pre-arranged meetings, with a prepared agenda circulated in advance. These might be board meetings, project planning meetings, budget review meetings, etc.
- **Ad Hoc** – usually arranged at very short notice. There is no prepared agenda and people have had very little time, if any, to prepare. An example of this is a meeting in response to a crisis or a meeting with clients when a formal agenda might be seen as rigid.
- **Problem Solving** – the aim of these meetings is to generate ideas to overcome or take advantage of a given set of circumstances.
- **Information Sharing** – this is when people get together to share information and update one another. This may take the form of the Monday morning departmental meeting or a work-in-progress meeting.

The purposes and styles of these meetings are all different. They will require a different style of chairperson, different room layout and different sets of minutes. However, there are some general factors we should consider when planning for and conducting meetings. These will help ensure that the meeting is time well spent.
- **Purpose** – fundamental to the success of any meeting. All meetings should have a clear and forward-looking purpose. This should take the form of a single statement incorporating the words 'in order to':

    'We are here today in order to agree ...'

    'We are here today in order to allocate tasks for ...'

    Avoid the word 'because' – it usually has negative implications. e.g :

'We are here because we always meet on a Friday.'

'We are here because there is a crisis in the factory.'

Concentrate your efforts on finding solutions rather than focusing on problems.

Even if you are not chairing the meeting you should have a personal purpose for attending the meeting. You should clarify this in your own mind before you go to the meeting. If you cannot think of a personal purpose for attending, then don't! Whilst it might be nice to attend, if you are not gaining any personal benefit you could probably use the time more effectively.

- **Preparation** – this naturally follows on from a clear purpose statement. Without that it is very difficult to plan. For those important meetings, you should always plan preparation time in your diary well ahead of the meeting. Use this time to clarify your thoughts, gather the necessary materials and think through your arguments.

  It is useful to have a special book for planning meetings or if you use a loose leaf time-planning system, have a section in there for meetings. The moment you arrange the meeting or receive notice of it start a new page for the meeting. It may not be for another week or two but this will give you an opportunity to plan your thoughts and jot down points you want to make at the meeting as you think of them. Take the pages to the meeting and note down all the decisions. This will save you having to wait for the minutes which may not appear for some time after the meeting.

- **Agenda** – an accurate agenda circulated in good time prior to the meeting is a tremendous help to all those attending. The items should be in logical order and not a simple 'shopping list' of items but a clear statement of what you aim to achieve from each item.

  The items on the agenda should be kept to a reasonable number to allow full discussion within the time available. Remember meetings have a life span of about 45 minutes to 1 hour. People soon switch off after this. The power of the discussion and decision-making suffers.

- **People** – the attendees for a meeting should be driven by the agenda. If delegates are only required for certain items it may be cost effective to group these together and then invite them in only for the relevant section of the meeting. Remember the more people you have at the meeting the longer it is likely to last. Everyone should have a clearly understood function if their presence at the meeting is to be beneficial.

- **Environment** – a key issue if the meeting is to be a success. This is never noticed when it is right but can destroy a meeting when it is wrong. Some of the things that should be considered are:

Room	– size and shape
	– temperature
	– facilities
Furniture	– some chairs are most uncomfortable
	– do you require a round table, square table, U-shape – they all create a different atmosphere
Visual aids	– make sure they are there and working
	– try them out beforehand
Creature comforts	– coffee/biscuits/refreshments – when and how are they going to be served.

- **Timings** – ensure that your meetings have both a published start and finish time. These should be known and agreed by all. Start on time but late-comers should be welcomed with as little fuss as possible. If you have six people in a meeting and it starts ten minutes late you have just lost your company one hour. Convert this to money and you are eating into your profit margins!

   Think about the best time of day for the meeting. Immediately after lunch and at the end of the day are probably not the best times if you want people to be fresh and alert.

- **Minutes** – these are the responsibility of the person chairing the meeting although they should avoid taking them. Appoint somebody well in advance. They may need training on how to take minutes which is a skill in itself. The person taking the minutes should not be expected to play an active part in the discussion.

Meetings are often longer and less precise than they need to be simply because their purpose has not been clearly defined. With a clear purpose it is easier to have:

- fewer items on the agenda
- fewer people at the meeting

- a clearer idea of how long the meeting will take
- better preparation by delegates, making their contribution more succinct and positive

Meetings are about team work – we all have a responsibility to ensure they are effective use of time.

CHAPTER THREE

GOAL SETTING AND PRIORITIZING

'If you don't know where you are going, the chances are you will end up somewhere else.'

HOW many times have you got in to your car, got on a bus or a train without a firm idea of where you wanted to end up? Very rarely I suspect, yet all too often people squander their precious resources of time and energy by working with no clear idea of their goals. Without a goal to focus on it is impossible to prioritize effectively, or make adjustments to maintain the most effective course towards achieving it.

GOALS

Goals should give you a clear indication of where you want to be at a given point in time. You can have short, medium and long-term goals but the principles behind goal setting remain the same.

PURPOSE OF GOALS

- To focus your attention.
- To give you a time framework in which to plan.
- To help motivate yourself and others.
- To ensure everybody is clear about what is happening.
- To help reward yourself when the task is complete.

THE SETTING OF GOALS

When setting goals you should follow this sequence:
- See it ...
- Say it ...
- Write it down ...
- Do it ...

See it ...
'To have a dream to strive for is to make life worth living.'

If you have a picture in your mind of where you want to be at the end of the day, month or whatever period, it will help put things into perspective and give you encouragement to keep going. People of vision and imagination strive for goals that others can merely admire or envy. Your goals are often only limited by your imagination.

Say it ..., Write it ...
Verbalizing and then writing down your goals is a commitment to yourself and others. If you tell others about your goals they too can help and support you. If you write your goals down you have committed them to paper and are more likely to achieve them. The more clearly you see your goals, the more likely you are to achieve them.

Here is a simple mnemonic for setting yourself clear goals.

M =	Measurable	Have quantitative and qualitative criteria for your goals.
A =	Achievable	If you set yourself impossible goals you will only become demotivated and stop setting them. Equally by setting a goal too far into the future you are in danger of losing sight of it before it is achieved. Alternatively do not make your goals so simple that they fail to challenge you.
S =	Specific	The more clearly you can visualize your goal the greater will be your motivation to achieve it.
T =	Time	Set yourself a deadline to drive for. Without some limit on time there is unlikely to be any sense of urgency in your work.

By setting yourself goals using the MAST formula you have taken the first step towards increasing your productivity, particularly in areas where you are either frightened or bored.

HAVE TO VS WANT TO

The most effective goals are set by ourselves rather than being imposed by others. This way they relate to things you **want** to achieve rather than those you **have** to.

By setting yourself the right 'want to' goals in as many areas of work as possible you are far less likely to find others imposing 'have to' goals upon you. Your standing in your organization will be that of a free man, not a slave or automaton, and you will be training yourself to have the kind of initiative that is an essential requirement as you progress up the management ladder.

ACHIEVING YOUR GOALS

Once you have set goals you need to achieve them. It is up to you to take the responsibility to make it happen.

- **Be positive** – if you have set achievable goals you know you can do them. Think of the rewards of success rather than the penalties of failure. This approach allows you to use winning self-talk and fuels the desire to achieve your goals.
- **Be firm but flexible** – single-minded determination is a good quality when striving to achieve goals. It is an even better quality when you are flexible and adaptable in your approach.
- **Be creative** – there may be many ways of achieving the same goal. Lateral and creative thinking and searching for variables can overcome high obstacles. Listen and be willing to learn from others.
- **Be patient** – if at first you do not succeed, then try again. Learn from your mistakes, take a fresh look at your plans and re-focus if necessary.

Goal setting is both necessary and fun. On a daily basis you should aim to set yourself no more than three goals. Any more than that and it starts to become a 'to do list'.

This process can be applied to many other aspects of your life. Some other areas you might set goals for are:

- Your family life
- Your social life
- Your leisure activities
- Your sporting life
- Your house

I am sure we all have gardens, bathrooms or spare rooms we have been intending to do something about for ages. What about that foreign language you have been meaning to learn for the last few years? A goal of a cassette tape a week for the next ten weeks will certainly make a start!

EXERCISE IN GOAL SETTING

Set one work and one non-work goal for the short, medium and long term. Remember 'MAST'.

Short-Term – within the next week

Work Goal _____

_____

Non-work Goal _____

_____

Medium-Term – within the next 2 months

Work Goal _____

_____

Non-work Goal _____

_____

Long-Term – within the next year

Work Goal _____

_____

Non-work Goal _____

_____

Now plan the various action steps which need to be done to achieve the goals and write them in your diary.

PRIORITIZING

Once you have set your goals and are clear about what you want to achieve, you are in a much better position to prioritize your tasks.

MEDIUM- TO LONG-TERM PRIORITIES

In order to prioritize your tasks in work, you need to be clear about what the purpose of your job is. This may require you going back to your job description or even writing one if you have not got one. You should constantly update your job description in light of changing responsibilities. The job description you were given two years ago may bear little resemblance to what you actually do today.

Once you have clarified the purpose of your job you can set the goals you need to achieve that purpose. The Key Performance Areas (KPAs) are the major categories of things you do to meet these goals. The areas will vary from job to job, but usually fall into about six main headings.

To help you be clear on how you should use your time effectively, it is important to prioritize this list. A list of KPAs prioritized might look something like this:

Sales	Priority 1
Administration	Priority 5
Budgeting	Priority 3
Personnel Management	Priority 2
Attending Conferences	Priority 6
Training Others	Priority 4

The activities are all the things that we do on a daily basis under these various areas.

e.g. Sales – Looking for new clients
– Cold calling
– Presentations
– Maintaining client data base
– Arranging client lunches

This exercise will give you an overall impression of how you should be using your time. In the above example, if you are regularly spending 60 per cent of your time on administration and only 10 per cent on sales then you need to look again at how you are using your time.

DAILY PRIORITIZING OF TASKS

Whilst it is important to maintain a watching brief on how you use your time on a medium to long-term basis, it is just as important to prioritize your tasks on a daily basis. A very easy way is to divide your tasks into high, medium and low priority tasks.

High priority
Important and urgent work that has to be completed on time and any delay has to be avoided. High priority work is top priority work.

Medium priority
Equally important work but which has a longer term deadline. This is important work, but not imminent. But today's medium priority work can becomes next week's or next month's high priority!

Low priority
Non-important work that can generally be delayed, deferred, scrapped, screened out, or delegated to assistants.

In the business of everyday life the high priority and low priority tasks usually get done – high priority because they have to be done; low priority because they are quick five-minute jobs that we can easily do. It is nearly always the medium priority tasks which get squeezed out. Yet it is those tasks which help us to become proactive and successful. It is even more important when we are working on medium priority tasks that we apply all the good time management principles.

CHAPTER FOUR

TIME PLANNING

'Most people don't plan to fail – they just fail to plan.'

HAVING worked out your goals, successful planning will help you achieve them. Many people find planning boring or claim they don't have enough time, others spend all their time planning and little time doing! Whatever your approach to planning, it is worth taking some time out to ensure that the job is achieved to the right standard and on time. Planning is your time to think through some of the detail. Planning should be both fun and flexible – fun because you are planning into the future and the unknown, flexible because you need to be able to cope with the changes that lie ahead.

A BALANCED APPROACH

Time planning will vary greatly from job to job and person to person. We can liken ourselves to a young tree we plant in the garden. That tree must have some roots firmly planted in the ground, but the part that is above the ground must be flexible enough to bend and sway depending on the weather. If that tree has no roots it will simply blow away or fall down at the first sign of wind or rain. Likewise, if the part above ground is rigid and inflexible the first rush of wind or rain will snap it. Our time planning should be just the same. We need some planning, something to give us stability, but we also need flexibility to cope with the problems and distractions that crop up all the time. No planning, no roots and we will get blown away with the first problems, too much planning and we will not be able to react and respond effectively to issues as they occur. As with many things in life, a balance is required. Invest some time in planning at the start and it will pay dividends later on.

Assuming you are clear about your goals you need to work out two things:

● What percentage of your time can you plan
● How far ahead you can effectively plan

A person in a highly reactive job may only be able to plan as little as one third of their time and may be only a few weeks in advance. Somebody in a less reactive job can probably plan much more, perhaps half their time, and further ahead.

LEVELS OF PLANNING

For all of us there are effectively three levels of planning. The time frame in which they are effective will vary and you must work this out for your own job. The levels should work like a funnel focusing in on the short term. The short term is the product of all your other planning.

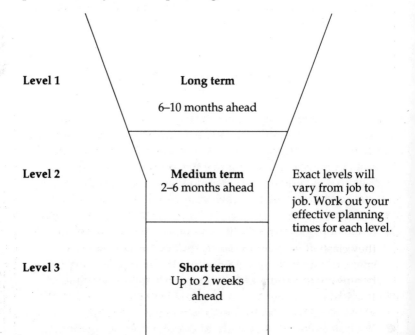

Level 1 — Long term — 6–10 months ahead

Level 2 — Medium term — 2–6 months ahead — Exact levels will vary from job to job. Work out your effective planning times for each level.

Level 3 — Short term — Up to 2 weeks ahead

You should have the facility in your diary or planning tools to help you plan at each level.

MEDIUM TO LONG-TERM PLANNING

- Identify your long-term goals. This will give you a sense of purpose and direction.
- Break large goals down into smaller more manageable chunks. Give each chunk a start and a finish time and plan these in your diary.
- Use your imagination to work out the various options and possibilities.
- Review your performance regularly and modify your plan accordingly. The main goals are unlikely to change but the ways of achieving them, i.e. the planning, may.
- Don't over-plan or over-commit yourself. This is a certain way of not achieving your goals. Remember, if you think you can only plan about 40 per cent of your time, you should only be accounting for 40 per cent of time in your planning.
- Remain flexible in your planning.
- Use monthly/annual planning charts to help you plan (see page 40).
- When planning ahead in your diary don't just put in fixed appointments and meetings. Plan those other tasks which are going to be placing a demand on your time.
- The meetings and appointments are fixed; the other activities can be moved nearer the time. You must plan for the time the task will take you to give an overall impression of the demands on your time and other resources, e.g. computers, secretarial and support staff.
- You can then look ahead for priority clashes and problems.
- By planning ahead it might be easier to change deadlines if they clash. It is easier to change things, bring in help, or speak to clients three weeks before the event than keep going, hoping for the best and panicking close to the deadline.
- If you are over-committed it may be possible to delegate. The earlier you delegate, the better for all concerned.
- You can even out your highs and lows in terms of workloads. Our workloads can come in peaks and troughs; by looking

EXAMPLE OF MONTHLY PLANNING

DAY	MORNING		AFTERNOON	
1				
2			Budgets	H
3				
4	Meeting	M		
5				
			Appraisals	H
	SITE VISIT	H		
			Presentation Preparation	M
28	Project Meeting	H		
29				
30			Marketing Review	M

H = High Priority   **M** = Medium Priority   **L** = Low Priority

ahead to our busy periods we can bring work forward and start it earlier. Most of us push work away from us when we are busy. This builds brick walls further down the road. By looking ahead we can bring some of those bricks towards us.

● By having a fairly good picture of your workload over the next four weeks you are in a better position to say no to some of those additional tasks. It's not always possible but worth a try!

● If you prefer to see a week at a time rather than a month, use a series of weekly plans. Some people do this planning in their diary, some on a planning board, some on their computer. Wherever you do it, do it!

MEDIUM-TERM PLANNING EXERCISE

Try it for yourself.
- Select a project due in the next 2–4 months.
- Establish the due date.
- Break it down into steps.
- Allocate time per step.
- Put steps in a logical order.
- Add up times required to action all steps.
- Work out 'start' date.

SHORT-TERM PLANNING – THE DAY

However effective your long or medium-term planning is, it will fail if you don't ensure it happens on the day. Some people like to plan the day at the close of the previous day, some on the day and some not at all! The problem of not planning the day is that the day can end up managing you rather than you managing it.

For this exercise you need a page-a-day diary or a desk-top pad which gives you a framework of a day. When planning the day think about the following:
- Your own body clock. Most people perform better in the morning than in the afternoon and most people enter a low point immediately after lunch. Try to do those hefty jobs which require maximum concentration when you are at your best.
- Plan your day as far as possible but leave room for the unexpected. Set your goals and write them down. Remember to keep to a maximum of three goals per day.
- Give yourself planning time first thing in the morning to set up the day.
- Make a list of the things you have to do in your planning time. Prioritize these tasks and give them a start time.
- Block out 'Prime Time' in your diary. This will give you a window of time for yourself.
- Avoid back-to-back meetings. A late finish to the first meeting will have a domino effect on the rest.

- Build in travel time for meetings where necessary and give yourself 'debrief time' immediately after each meeting.
- Prioritize and batch your telephone calls and give yourself 'telephone time' according to these priorities.
- If you have a secretary, regularly spend a few minutes updating him or her on your plans.
- If you are required to read, give yourself periods of reading time on a regular basis. This may seem like a luxury but don't feel guilty – it is part of your job.
- Always try to finish the day on a positive note. This will send you home in a good mood and help you face tomorrow feeling good.
- Use lots of colour in your diary. Coloured highlighter pens make the day look more exciting and help to highlight different activities. Your diary is a reflection of your life, make it look exciting!

Although I have stressed the importance of planning, don't become a slave to your daily plan. It is only a guide and may require changing as the day progresses.

DAILY PLAN

A typical day may look like the chart opposite. It is this sort of planning you should do during your planning time.

You now have some guidance for planning the day. This needs to be tailored to your own style and job constraints. Using a blank daily page, plan your ideal day bearing the following in mind.

- When do you feel at your best during the day?
- When do you find it hardest to concentrate?
- Do you find it difficult to work after lunch? How long does this last for?
- When is the best time for you to meet with your secretary?
- When is the best time of day for Prime Time?
- Do you have any fixed tasks during the day, e.g. daily planning meeting, phone head office, etc.? These should go in your plan first and then work the rest around it.

Daily Plan

	Schedule	General To Do List	Priority	Done
0700		● Letter – J. Smith	H	
0730		● Speak – Michael re. Sales Conference	M	
0800		● Memo – new Health Scheme	H	
0830	Planning time	● Phone – Sun Hotel re. Xmas Party		
0900	Secretary time	● Collect photocopying	L	
0930		● Check tax with pay office	H	
1000	Marketing plan	● Book theatre tickets	H	
1030				
1100	Travel Time		H	
	Project meeting			
1130	Travel Time			
1200	Debrief	**Today's Goals:**		
1230	Telephoning time	● Finish Marketing Plan by 11.00		
1300	Lunch	● Phone J. Smith at 12.30		
1330	Complete monthly expenses	● Reach stage 4 of Monthly report by 4 p.m.		
1400				
1430	Monthly report			
1500				
1530				
1600				
1630	Filing time			
1700				
1730				
1800				

PRIME TIME

Most people tend to work in very short periods of time before they are interrupted, the phone rings or they have to go to a meeting. This tends to average out at about 15 minutes. This is made worse by the way some people's diaries work out. Because we do not arrange everything at the same time, we can end up with problems. What seemed easy to fit in our diary a month ago when it was empty, can end up being a problem by the time the day arrives.

Two days in our diary might look like this.

	5th		6th	
a.m.				
	Boss!	H		
	Team meeting	H	Sales Rep's Meeting	L
p.m.	Lunch with Mary	L		
	Brainstorming Session	M	Management Meeting	H
			Interviewing	H

H = High priority   **M** = Medium priority   **L** = Low priority

The meeting with the sales representative who managed to make an appointment from a cold call might not have appeared a problem when he called a month ago as there was nothing else

44

in the diary then. Time has moved on and there is now much more pressure. You now wish you had not agreed to see the rep.

It is therefore essential to prioritize tasks as you put them in the diary. The day has become fragmented with meetings. In addition to these meetings there are all the other day-to-day tasks. These end up getting slotted into the small gaps that appear here and there during the day. It will usually be the quick low priority tasks or the very urgent high priority tasks which fill these gaps. The longer, more medium priority work will get squeezed out.

To help reduce the effects of a fragmented day you should book blocks of time in your diary for you. I call these blocks Prime Time – they are yours and nobody should be allowed to steal them.

● Aim for a 2-hour block twice a week.
● Plan it in your diary when your diary begins to get busy.
● Once you have put it in the diary resist the temptation to cancel it if something else crops up. Obviously you must retain some flexibility but remember it is your 'Prime Time'.
● Try to reduce interruptions to a minimum:
    Close your door or find a quiet room.
    Get your phone calls held at the switchboard or covered by somebody else.
    If you work in an open plan office and cannot get away from your desk, put a sign on your desk letting everybody know you want to be left alone.
● Have a clear plan what you are going to do during your Prime Time. Set a goal and prepare yourself fully for the time. Two hours' Prime Time can easily be frittered away if you do not plan it properly.
● Make yourself available after your Prime Time for colleagues who have been waiting to see you.

You are not indispensable, very few problems cannot wait two hours. If you are required to do high quality work on time you have a right to have the time to do it. You might not know what you are going to do in your Prime Time when you entered it in your diary but you can be sure that when the day arrives you will have some important work which requires your undivided attention. You now have the time to do it.

CONTROLLING YOUR DIARY

As we have seen, the use of a diary and good time management go hand-in-hand. Poor diary management often leads to poor time management. It is important then that you consider the following points:

- Using a page-a-day diary will enable you to plan the day in some detail.
- Try to combine your 'to-do lists' with your diary. It will save you having pieces of paper all over the desk.
- Avoid back-to-back meetings and always plan travel time where necessary.
- Block out your committed time as soon as possible, e.g. holidays, major meetings, seminars, training courses, etc. Add the important deadlines to give yourself an accurate picture of how busy you actually are.
- Prioritize your tasks.
- Make use of Prime Time – book it ahead of yourself, and guard it jealously.
- Have a space to jot down good ideas as they occur – don't rely on your memory.
- Have key telephone numbers handy.
- Have a book or section in your diary system for planning meetings and recording the decisions.

CHAPTER FIVE

PERSONAL ORGANIZATION AND WORK FLOW

Y OU have now developed your working pattern, priorities and planned your tasks, making effective use of your diary. We now have to make it happen. Many things can get in the way of this, some outside our control, but some most definitely within our control. The three things which can get in the way of us achieving our plans on a daily basis are:
- interruptions from colleagues
- the telephone
- a badly organized or untidy work place

If you want to manage your time effectively you need a system for managing these three issues.

MANAGING INTERRUPTIONS

There are two things to consider here:
- preventing interruptions,
- limiting the damage once interrupted.

PREVENTING INTERRUPTIONS

- **Environment** – we are in danger of building in interruptions by the way we organize our office furniture. You may not have much control over this but you can think about the position of your desk and chairs:

    Desk – even in open plan offices some areas are worse than others. These tend to be near the photocopier, fax machine, coffee machine or toilets. If your desk is next to one of these areas, try to move it. If you cannot, at least try

to ensure that your back is towards these things so that you are less likely to get caught in other people breaks.
Chairs – having more than one chair around your desk is an invitation for someone to sit in it! Once people sit down it is much more difficult to get rid of them. Unless a chair is vital, remove it. Failing that, leave a book or papers on it when you want to be left alone.

- **Work practice** – tell people if you do not want to be disturbed, particularly during your Prime Time.
- **Receiving mail** – if your mail is delivered throughout the day have a point away from our desk where it is left so that you can collect the mail at a time convenient to you, not the postman. Very few people can ignore an unopened envelope when it lands on the desk, especially if it is marked 'Private and Confidential'.

LIMITING THE DAMAGE

- **Interruption procedure** – encourage the interrupters to start by stating what they want and how long it will take.
- **Use body language to control interruptions** – for those persistent interrupters who simply will not go away try:
  – Standing up when they come to your desk. If necessary walk round your desk and greet them. In most cases this will give them the message to 'go away'.
  – Perch on your desk if you are happy to chat for a few minutes – this tells them it is temporary and you can stand up when you have had enough.
  – Delay the interruption until later. If the interruption is lower priority than the work you are doing, fix a meeting for later. Try to arrange the meeting in their office so you can leave when you have had enough. This is especially important if the other person is a well-known socializer.

As long as we work together there will be interruptions. Plan on being interrupted and allow time in your day for the unexpected but manage it properly. Remember, too, that you could be an interruption to other people! Set a good example.

MANAGING THE TELEPHONE

The telephone is probably both the most useful and the most annoying of all office equipment. When looking at how you manage the phone it is useful to divide the subjects under two headings:
● Calls you make,
● Calls you take.

CALLS YOU MAKE

You are in control here – use it to your advantage.
● **Prioritize calls** – make your high priority calls when you are at your best, leave others until later.
● **Batch your calls** – this will put you in a telephone mood – your calls will be quicker, you will come across better and it will save interrupting yourself during the day.
● **Plan your calls** – jot down the key points you want to make before you pick up the phone.
● **Keep control of the call** – if the person or information is not available, *you* offer to call back at an agreed time.
● **Don't be left on hold** – you may like the music but it is a waste of time.
Other tips for making a good impression:
● **First impressions** – the first few seconds are vital. State who you are and the purpose of your call.
● **Stand up** – particularly with those difficult phone calls. It is not easy to sound in control in a submissive or neutral position, i.e. sitting.
● **Smile** – yes, even on the phone! You sound friendlier and more sincere when smiling.

CALLS YOU TAKE

Like other interruptions you need to manage the calls coming in:
● **Screen the calls** – where possible get someone to screen your calls, especially during Prime Time.
● **Priorities** – on receiving the call quickly prioritize the nature of it in relation to what you are working on. Higher priority – deal with it now; medium or lower priority – try to arrange a call back later.

- **Delegate** – do you need to take the call or can someone else in your team deal with it as effectively?

DESK ORGANIZATION

A recent survey in London showed that on average most office-based people spend 17½ days a year looking for paper! Not good use of time.

- A desk is a place to work and not store work.
- Your desk is a reflection of the way you work.
- Other people tend to treat your desk the way you treat it.

Here are a few tips to help you maintain a fairly tidy desk:

- **Desk Equipment** – if you are easily distracted by things around you – the phone, the computer keyboard, etc – you can help yourself to be more productive by moving these out of your immediate field of view, e.g. to a table at your side.
- **Paperwork** – the more paper on your desk the more inefficient you are likely to be. Devise a system for routing paper when it hits your desk.. Rather than have lots of pending trays, file things that are not to be dealt with today and have a bring forward system in your diary for the remainder. Do not simply shuffle through paperwork, make decisions as to what action you plan to do with each piece of paper. The choices are:

    Action – immediately/today

    Delegate – plan all delegation early

    File – use a simple filing system based on retrieval rather than storage. Give yourself filing as often as you need. Mark it in your diary as an appointment with you and the filing cabinet!

    Bin – much of the paper on your desk could be out of date or irrelevant. The first step to a tidy desk is to get rid of the rubbish. When you receive reading material, date it. If you have not read it within a month, bin it. You are kidding yourself if you think you will get round to reading it after a month.

- **Bin It Day!** – mark time in your diary once a month. Make this the time to have a major tidy up. If you don't attack your desk or office regularly it will build up to a mammoth task. Procrastination will set in and the job will never get done!

KEY ACTION PLAN

My ten action points from this section are:

	Action	Start Date
1		
2		
3		
4		
5		
6		
7		
8		
9		
10		

My review date two months from today is ....

If I have achieved this action plan my reward will be ....

PART TWO

MANAGING YOUR TIME FOR HOME-BASED WORKERS

THIS middle section is aimed at both beginners and current operators in the home-based working environment. It is designed to provide a few handy tips for anyone who is either about to take the plunge in working from home – whether you have been on a career break or have recently left an organization – or for anyone who is already in this particular boat and floundering under a sea of too many things to do and no time to do them!

WHAT WILL YOU GET OUT OF IT?

(or is it worth my time reading it?)

There are four main stages to this section:
● The job search stage
● Starting up operations
● Up and running
● Keeping going

Each stage has a brief description of the main difficulties people encounter when trying to manage their time at home, followed by some ideas on potential solutions – all highly practical.

The sections are illustrated with real life situations experienced by individuals who have actually faced these problems and have tried out the solutions. Each solution will be followed by a time management lesson designed to sum up the main learning point of the examples preceding it.

At the end of each section you will find a draft action plan showing the main points and tasks to work on in order to achieve a more effective use of your time in relation to the particular problem just explored.

The section concludes with ten time controllers for easy reference (when you have a spare moment!).

A QUICK OVERALL VIEW
OF THE HOME-BASED WORKER

Home-based workers come in all shapes and sizes, just the same as company-based workers and they encounter exactly the same difficulties but very often more intensely, for reasons we shall explore further on.

You may be someone who has been made redundant after some years with a company and who now finds themselves at home working on the job search. Or you may have decided that going into another company role is not for you and that working from home on a self-employed consultancy basis or as a small limited company is what you now want to do with your life. So you are exchanging one type of schedule with plenty of structure and externally imposed regulations for complete independence where you alone will control, decide and manage your own income-generating activities.

No matter how big or small your home-based operation, you will come up against the need to manage your time. Within companies this is often done for you by colleagues screaming for information, by customers demanding rapid response or by committee deadlines by which the report simply *must* be ready.

At home most of these pressures are a lot further away and may seem almost invisible at times. This means you will need to develop a strong sense of self-discipline if you are consistently to find the next job or project, complete it, receive the money for it and make sure there is another income generator to follow up.

When you were in an organization at least you could only be called upon by people associated with the job. Now you will have the job and domestic environment pulling you in different directions at the same time with no 5.30 p.m. closing time. You may think you will be master or mistress of your own time with no trivial interruptions from colleagues to distract you from the main task. But in the next four chapters we shall look at some of the home-based time-gobblers that can stand between you and the regular income generation you need.

CHAPTER SIX

JOB SEARCH

S O you have decided at long last to take the plunge and move to a completely different job. Or, and this is sadly much more common, like thousands of other people in the 1990s you have been given no choice about working elsewhere and now need – as a matter of urgency – to start a full-scale job-search campaign.

What immediate obstacles are you going to meet? If you have been made redundant then you will first need to deal with the trauma of being effectively rejected by the organization for which you have been working for a certain length of time, be it two months or twenty years. All changes are painful and this particular shock treatment is more fundamental than most.

So how can time management principles help you in setting out towards success in the next stage of working life? Like every plan of campaign you must have objectives and targets to aim for. If you don't know where you are going it is highly unlikely you will get there – or know if you have arrived!

So the first thing is to take this campaign very seriously and use time limits to make sure you keep your nose to the grindstone.

STEP 1

Set your target (getting the job)
Time limit: say three months.

STEP 2

Prepare a three-month plan
    You may think (or hope) that you will be tucked away nicely by the end of two weeks with a new job, but this is a hard world

and there are a lot of job seekers to compete with out there. Hopefully these ideas will give you that 'competitive edge' and put you back confidently in the money-making classes quicker.

THREE-MONTH PLAN

Objective	Time
Obtain a *suitable* new job	3 months

Tasks

Week 1	Get over the trauma (maybe a complete break). DSS/DE registration. Self-analysis – what do I really want to do.
Week 2	DSS/DE follow-up. Start CV. Keep a check on the press for adverts. Financial reorganization.
Week 3	Continue work on CV. Start work on contacts list.
Week 4	Visit reference library. Complete CV.

TO BE CONTINUED WEEKLY

STEP 3

Make up a DAILY THINGS TO DO LIST

Day	Daily Tasks
1	Get the job search campaign equipped – stationery, workplace, newspapers, telephone
2	Go swimming Visit DSS Go to a meeting of your Trade Association/Professional Institute if relevant

3	Contact bank manager Check papers for jobs

4	Play football Write applications

5	Attend committee – Parent Teachers Association Visit reference library

Of course it's not enough just to write these plans in beautiful script. You have to follow them! And if you find things aren't getting done, you need to revise the plans – probably adding in the endless little tasks that you never even thought about when you were cocooned in your company, but more of that in a while.

Perhaps a few hints on how to work out who you are and what you have to offer are needed – the result of this exercise will show you how much time is required to prepare yourself for the new job before you even start looking.

A TIME-CONSUMING
BUT RESULT-ORIENTED TECHNIQUE

What we are looking at is a marketing approach to the competitive job market so you will need to adopt some marketing tools, or, to put it quite simply, the marketing approach to launching a new product which is what you are doing!

SWOT ANALYSIS

SWOT stands for **S**trengths, **W**eaknesses, **O**pportunities and **T**hreats. All you do is list your strengths and weaknesses so you know what you have to sell to the marketplace (the employers) and what you want to avoid or at least be able to minimize! e.g :

Strengths
- 'A' levels/degree/professional qualification.
- Experience of particular jobs or types of product or service.

- Language skills.
- Driving licence.
- Ability to travel.
- Leadership skills.
- Communication skills.

Weaknesses
- Frequent job changes in the past.
- Must stay in locality.
- No formal qualifications.

Now the
Opportunities – or where you can sell these skills:
- In the same type of company.
- Moving the same skills to a completely different type of organization, e.g. many skills such as administration skills are transferable and can be used equally well in the private, public or charity sectors.
- Teaching your expertise.
- Doing something completely different, e.g. emigrating, setting up a small business connected with one of your leisure activities.

Lastly the
Threats – or the things that will hinder your job search:
- Financial commitments may mean you need to find a job very quickly and therefore you cannot easily do something very different from what you know.
- There may be many competitors in the market you want to get into – so you need to be sure that you have a special edge.

WEEK 1

Once you have completed your Self-Analysis, you are ready to start the job search proper.

Begin Work on your CV
As soon as you have quizzed yourself with lots of questions about what you like, what you are good at, what you hate, what you are bad at, etc, you can then start putting together your CV which is how you tell the world about yourself.

You will need at least two or three attempts at this, so don't be surprised to see this task down in Week 2 as well and probably Week 3. If you get this 'product brochure' right, you will find the selling job much easier.

Read the newspapers for adverts
Locally/nationally/internationally, depending on your SWOT analysis results. If you can only work within a 10-mile radius because you have no car, then don't waste time reading the International edition of the *Sunday Times*.

Make a start on your network list
These are the people who may know of an opportunity that you would not necessarily find out about. You need to draw up a list of all the possible sources of this type of information, including friends, colleagues/former colleagues, customers, suppliers, family, etc.

Next week you can start to ring them or write letters and ask their advice in your job search. This all takes time as you are now beginning to realize so you will need to allocate time to write, post and follow up letters.

This has probably taken care of the first week so now you can plan week 2.

WEEK 2

Day	Daily Tasks
1	Revisit DSS/DE Continue work on CV
2	Visit the library's reference section to find out the information available
3	Visit friend/colleague to maintain contacts See bank manager
4	Review papers to check any jobs worth applying for
5	Visit exhibition to keep up to date with new products/ contacts

This detailed monthly/weekly/daily plan is designed to ensure that you make the most of the time available to you and achieve your goal as quickly as possible. With this plan you simply substitute your old fixed employer-imposed timetable with one that suits you and helps you achieve your goal despite the huge gap your loss of job has brought.

Let us take a few **THEN** and **NOW** scenarios to put the difficulties in context and provide a few solutions.

SCENARIO 1

No framework or structure:

Then

For the past x number of years you have been clocking in to the company system or at least conforming to the standard company working hours, such as 9 a.m. to 5.30 p.m.

Now

Nobody – be it time-clock, siren, supervisor or colleague-pressure – is there to force or encourage you to turn up at any pre-set time.

Result: you may (especially in chilly winter months) decide to turn over and have a lie-in and end up spending the best part of the day between warm sheets – very comfortable but not very productive!

It is a competitive market-place out there and if you are not up and about in it you will be another late bird who missed the worm!

Exercise 1

Keep a check on what time you get up and what you do in the first three hours of your day for a couple of weeks just to make sure you're not drifting into gentle stagnation.

If you have always been used to getting up at 6.30 a.m. then your personal time clock is not going to change overnight. So make good use of this time. Maybe you can take the dog for a walk and save someone else the trouble. And then you will get a chance to scan the paper for useful information or even job adverts before that same dog or someone else mangles the vital pages. Or, in the summer months, there is the ideal opportunity to get cracking on the neglected garden – just think of the compliments that may ensue, or even the delicious fresh vegetables you can proudly dish up.

Do remember not to extend this new-found extra time beyond strict limits. Your next job – the job search campaign – must have the same working hours you have just left.

SCENARIO 2

No support systems

Then
Although you may have been a great achiever in your last job, just how much of the work did you actually do yourself and how much did you rely on other colleagues? How often did you pick up the phone to someone in another location, pop down to the next floor to get assistance from another department or just ask your secretary to go and get a document?

Now
You have to do it all yourself. OK, it gives you the freedom to organize your own time but it does not give you any support in putting things together.

Exercise 2
Write down a list – and it could be a surprisingly long one – of all the documents, items of equipment and sources of information you need to start selling yourself into this new marketplace.

To get you started: pens, paper, envelopes, etc. These are not in the stationery storecupboard now. You have to go down to the shops and buy them.

Contacts who may be the key to where your new job is coming from are not necessarily available on the end of the phone at the drop of a hat. You have to go and make sure you talk to and see them. You have to keep calling them back – you are now your own secretary.

Writing applications is time-consuming and hard enough – but then you can't just drop the letter in the out-tray. You have to go to the post box (having bought the stamps) and without doubt the first time you will miss the last collection because nobody was there to remind you about it. Let's hope you don't miss the closing date for the job applications!

SCENARIO 3

No colleagues or social side of work

We all know that in fact the real reason for going to work is to keep the bank manager at bay but what about the voluntary workers who turn up day after day for no financial reward? And did you know that over 50 per cent of couples meet through work? And what about all those sports and social clubs, not to mention the Christmas party?

Then
The first thing you did when you arrived in the morning was exchange pleasantries with your colleagues – what you did last night, the weather, the kids, etc. And that carried on throughout the day as you met different people. In addition were the formal meetings where actual work matters were discussed, not always in an entirely formal way but with a good deal of social chit-chat to help the medicine go down.

Now
Once the people you live with have gone off to their daily activities (school, factory, hospital, shops, etc) you are left all alone. No one to communicate with except the wallpaper and possibly the postperson. No one to boast about a success to or commiserate with over a failure. No one to share your fears, moans or joys.

Exercise 3
Try to list the total number of people you came into contact with on an average day at work – from the moment you arrived at the gatepost to the time you left the building. Include both informal and formal chats and you will be amazed how much time you spent in social contact. Not all of it was pleasant maybe and probably a good proportion of it was not essential but your day would certainly have been empty without it.

Now make another list and record every contact with people you have during the day at home when you are doing your job/ project search. Is there a big difference in the number and length of the contacts?

A few examples:
● **Family:** general family business – getting people off to their

daily activities, making transport arrangements, meal organization, etc.

- **General traders:** post deliverers, milkmen, market researchers, Jehovah's witnesses, etc – some of these are of potential assistance in getting a job but most are in fact eating into your job search campaign time.
- **Well-meaning friends:** general chit-chat.

It's essential to keep up your social circle, partly because someone in it may hold the key to your next job, but you need to keep a close eye on the amount of time these little friendly exchanges take. Try to allocate a specific amount of time to this social support each week and don't let it over-run.

SCENARIO 4

No discipline

Then

Everyone has jobs that must be done but which they tend to leave to last, half hoping they will go away. Of course they never disappear completely, but sometimes colleagues lent a hand, or at the very least someone bent your ear and forced you to do it either by encouragement or threats.

Now

There is only you involved in the job search, so *you* will have to do all the boring/difficult/expensive/time-consuming tasks and bite the bullet. Otherwise it will never get done and the whole operation could fall flat and you will be without work for a few more weeks or months.

Exercise 4

List all the things you really hated doing at work and tried to avoid or leave until last. Be honest! It might be writing letters, making phone calls to people you don't know, keeping tidy records or checking through final drafts of reports. Now make a space in each day or week for actually doing those tasks – because if you don't there's no one else to push you into doing them!

MUST DO but HATE TO DO LIST

Description	Time Needed
Following up applications with a phone call	4 x 15 minutes per day

This may seem a lot but how often do you get through to the person you want first time around?

And don't forget to make a note of previous conversations to ensure you are ready when they phone you back with an invitation to an interview.

Keeping job search file tidy, including the new jobs, letters and notes	30 minutes per day

Making and drinking coffee, etc, including lunch and tea	90 minutes per day

Don't forget the time needed to pop to the shops when there's no bread left for that quick sandwich. And then discovering that it's early closing day so you have to go somewhere else!

Library Research	1 day per week

Updating yourself on companies, people or products so you can decide what to apply for or what to ask at interviews.

SCENARIO 5

Your impact on the family

Then
You went out early in the morning and came back late at night and sometimes you didn't see the rest of the family from Sunday night until Friday night. Perhaps that was a good thing or perhaps you regretted it and now feel that you will be able to spend so much more time with them – helping out with homework, washing up, or cooking the occasional meal. Beware!

The family has managed quite well thank you in your absence – they have got into their own routines and ways of doing things and everything works well until you start appearing on the scene hoping to pick up the threads and provide what you see as valuable assistance.

Now
You are available for large parts of the day and one of two things can happen to cause your job search to go badly wrong. Either you will create absolute havoc and upset everyone by insisting on imposing your own routine and forcing other people to change theirs, or you will give up trying to fit in and feel like an unwanted intrusion hanging about the place, getting more and more frustrated.

Exercise 5
Observe over a week exactly how your place of residence functions – who does what and when. Identify if and where you can help – not where you want but where they express a need. Discuss your new home-based role for the duration of the job search and take on board the ideas of those around you for occupying your time constructively.

The opposite side of this problem is of course getting dragged into all those small but arduous tasks you have been promising to do for months but never quite found the time!

If you have a sensible and constructive time plan you can avoid spending (wasting?) time in activities which will not help towards your real goal of further employment. However, it can also be a chance to join in more domestic ratters and by contributing to family life you will reduce any tendency to see yourself as useless just because you have lost your job. But keep these activities in their rightful place in your overall time plan.

CHAPTER SEVEN

STARTING UP

Time Management Diary	
Take the time to decide your objectives	Now
Review the targets	Monthly/weekly
Take time to analyse your strengths and weaknesses	Now
Calculate time needed to do it all yourself	Now
Review this in the light of experience	Weekly
Keep an eye on the costs	Daily
Organize yourself around the family	Daily/weekly

THIS chapter is designed to provide time management hints for those who have taken the decision to go it alone and work in their chosen field from home. This may be as a self-employed consultant or running a small business – in either set-up, the time management lessons are the same.

The difficulties you face can be set out as follows:

DIFFICULTY: No organizational framework to give you a sense of purpose or trigger you into action.

Solution 1
Set yourself some objectives to establish where you are heading – because unless you know that, you have no chance of getting there (or knowing when you have arrived).

You could start with an estimate of your required annual income based on what you have been spending until now. Don't make the mistake of thinking you can cut your spending by half – you may for a short while but some things are essential and if you are working hard you need to have some relaxation which also needs to be paid for. Break this annual amount down into monthly chunks of earnings and work out what you need to do each week to achieve that level of income per month. Finally, decide and write down what these weekly and monthly goals mean in terms of daily tasks, for example:

Annual income target   £40000
Monthly earnings   £ 3333
Weekly earnings   £   833
How many products/contracts/assignments is this?

Solution 2
Take time to decide what you are trying to achieve before you waste a lot of energy and time running in unproductive directions. Prepare charts for monthly, weekly and daily targets and keep them right under your nose so you can't forget them! This detailed plan will ensure you know where you are in relation to your end goal at all times. Then you can either take a kick up the backside to spur you on to greater effort or hopefully allow yourself a pat on the back because you're doing better than expected.

Keep referring to your plan – tick off when you have achieved things and change the targets if they're too hard or easy. Make sure you include all the activities you need to do in order to achieve your goals – remember the things you don't like doing but know you must!

This part of getting started on working from home is absolutely crucial – if your plans are inaccurate you will either not get everything done or find you have time and no money on your hands. Involve the whole domestic contingent in your objectives – they will profit and lose by your activities!

TIME MANAGEMENT LESSON 1
Take time at the beginning to find out where you are going.

DIFFICULTY: No colleagues or other departments to call to get things done for you.

Solution
To get round the lack of support system and infrastructure, you need to identify which tasks you can handle yourself and those where you need help. The ones you don't like will inevitably take you longer so you must allow for that. You can either force yourself to do them or buy in some help from outside – but this will cost you hard-earned money and you will also have to spend time making sure the paid help does the work properly.

Task implications	Skill source	Time
Typing letters	self	slow at keyboard – training course?
	subcontract	availability?
Filing	self	1 hour per week
Cold calls	self	1 day per week
Equipment purchase	self	2 days per month
Post	self	½ hour per day
Bank	self	1 day per 2 months

A strengths and weaknesses chart will help you decide which tasks you should spend time on and which are better farmed out – always remembering the cost of subcontracting and the additional time needed to supervise the quality of any service you do not undertake personally.

TIME MANAGEMENT LESSON 2
Allow enough time for all the extra tasks that you now have to do yourself.

DIFFICULTY: Money needed to start up operations before you start earning.

There will be certain expenses in running the business that you have to pay out for on an ongoing basis and before any income is brought in. You have to sow pennies to reap pounds.

Solution 1
Check out the most cost-effective (not necessarily the cheapest) way of providing whatever services you need.

For instance in buying computer equipment always go for the best you can afford to do the job you need doing, not only now but when your business expands which may be sooner than you think. Everyone knows of people who buy a cheap photocopier on special offer just to start them off only to find it produces just two copies per minute and that means a long time for 50 A4 letters.

Solution 2
And what about doing some tasks when they are cheaper rather than as soon as they come into your head. Make your phone calls after 1 p.m. – it's up to 40 per cent cheaper. And why not send fax messages after 6 p.m. – even cheaper. The only people you can't do that to are banks, because they are not allowed to leave fax machines on overnight for security reasons.

Solution 3
Use the morning to write letters, file, buy stationery, etc – if you can't phone people then make sure you are using your time effectively.

TIME MANAGEMENT LESSON 3
Do what you can when you can.

DIFFICULTY: No personal office space.

You were perhaps used to a full office, or at least a desk, chair, dedicated terminal, phone, etc, all kept in reasonable working order by cleaners, secretary and colleagues. Now, however, you have to negotiate time and space with other users in the home.

The teenage daughter who is never off the phone – either receiving or making calls? Or the student son who, whilst you are delighted to see him home from college, just happens to occupy the only room where you can put the filing cabinet and of course can see no reason for getting up at 8 a.m. during the vacation just to let you look for papers you need to take for a client meeting. Or the bright young twins who are delighted with the new PC and invite all their friends round to play the latest video games?

These are not only space but time management problems.

Solution
Rearrange your day/week to take account of domestic constraints on your activities – try negotiating hours for the use of the phone (or invest in another line), agree reasonable access hours to your office equipment and think ahead and retrieve your important papers the night before.

TIME MANAGEMENT LESSON 4
Your time is inextricably bound up with other people's.

DIFFICULTY: Getting all the contracts set up.

You have identified your strengths and weaknesses in terms of all the support services you need to get your product or services out of the door and on to the market, so the next stage is to set up the contracts you need to achieve this. You can do the expert bits – but someone or something else has to do the tedious or difficult bits. And you must take time to get these sorted properly or all your expertize will go to waste.

Solution
List out all the organizations/individuals/services you need to have in place before you are ready to go into full operation.

You might have thought of some of these:
- Bank/building society account
- VAT registration
- Income tax status change
- Social Security contributions change
- Stationery purchases – paper, envelopes, pens, paper clips etc

- Office equipment – word processor, PC, photocopier, fax machine, answerphone
- Furniture – chair, desk, phone, filing cabinet
- Research materials – books, papers, journals
- Car servicing – no more passing it to the Fleet Manager and getting a replacement from the pool.

And those are just for starters – wait until you are up and running!

Just take a few seconds for each of the above items and work out the following:

- Where can I get this?
- When can I do it?
- How long will it take me to look at one alternative?
- Do I need to compare prices and services?

TIME MANAGEMENT LESSON 5
Don't forget the time needed to organize the rest of the world into contributing to your business.

TIME MANAGEMENT LESSON 6
You don't just do these things once – they need time to cultivate/install/repair and replace.

It's OK when you can just get the office services department to call the photocopier engineer but when you have to look up the number and find that you are not actually a major customer like your old firm and therefore they will only be in your area on the only day next week that you have already organized a client meeting ...

ACTION PLAN FOR THE STARTING UP PHASE

- Make up a business plan incorporating annual earnings and breakdown of activities needed to achieve that figure.
- Give yourself realistic timescales for each stage of each activity.
- Calculate the time needed to deal with the rest of the world both in and outside the home.

CHAPTER EIGHT

UP AND RUNNING

Time Management Diary

Take time to do your research	Twice a week
Keep up with your profession/trade	Weekly
Keep the office tidy	Daily
Keep on top of your subject	Weekly
Don't spend too long chatting	Daily

O K, so you have got off the ground. In fact you have just completed your first assignment – given to you by your old employer just to get you started. And now you're sitting in your well-equipped office at home all ready to respond to the hundreds of new customers about to beat a path to your door. Can you hear the thunder of their footsteps? No?

What you need to do is identify where those customers are and make contact with them.

DIFFICULTY: Researching the marketplace.

You need to know who will buy your product at the price you are going to want to sell it and when they will want it.

Solution 1
Do desk research in the library – make regular visits to your local reference library, cultivate the Information Assistant there

and he/she will open a whole new world of information, directories, on-line terminals, etc from which you can glean vital clues not only about customers but about your competitors as well.

Solution 2
Daily reading of the Business Pages in the local and national press – not the sport or leisure pages! They are not likely to produce much income unless you are working in one of those sectors. You can impress customers with your knowledge of the latest innovations or personnel changes simply by taking 15–30 minutes every day to keep yourself informed.

Solution 3
Keep up to date with your professional or trade press. You are no longer on the office circulation list for all those documents you so often filed in the bin, but now you need them. It may take a lot of persistence with uninterested or inefficient circulation departments but get registered with the main publications that people in your business read or look at for information. You may find clues as to potential customers or product developments.

TIME MANAGEMENT LESSON 1
Build in reading time to your calendar.

DIFFICULTY: 'I never see anybody except the milkman and the postwoman.'

How often have you heard women who have been out of the employment market for a career break complain about how little professional or technical exchange they have had and how hard it is to get back into the world of jargons and buzz words?

Solution
Make a point of joining appropriate business contact sources at national and local level.
   Who are these sources?
● Chambers of Commerce
● Professional institutes
● Trade associations

- Conferences/exhibitions
- Self-help groups

Show yourself to be a regular attender. This is where you can get first-hand recent information about new developments, people, gossip and of course exchange experience with people in your business who are going through the same sorts of problems as you and may have just the answer or at least a few hints. You might also want to make a presentation about your business to the meeting and thus gain a captive audience and some free publicity.

TIME MANAGEMENT LESSON 2

Build professional contact time into your timetable – not so that it becomes a 'jolly' but enough to keep you aware of what is going on.

DIFFICULTY: You can never find that letter when someone rings up; you must get that proposal off tonight but you've run out of good quality paper or you need a short term overdraft to purchase an exceptional item but you can't get to see the Bank Manager before next week. Sounds familiar?

Solution 1
Plan ahead sufficiently to make sure you don't run out of paper or other essential items when it's early closing day.

Solution 2
Keep your filing under control before the piles of paper engulf you and your business prospects.

Solution 3
Make sure you have taken time to build up a good relationship with your bank so that they are willing to help you out in the odd emergency.

TIME MANAGEMENT LESSON 3

Build administrative time into your schedule.

DIFFICULTY: You are asked to present a paper at a national conference or to speak to your local Chamber of Commerce on an area of your business.

This could be the ideal opportunity for some free publicity and the chance to meet a highly specialist targeted audience. But – you were made redundant just as you were about to be sent on a public-speaking course and it's something you have never done – though you have seen and heard many disasters from the podium in your time ...

DIFFICULTY: You are in a highly technical business and are going to see one of the blue-chip companies in your field next month. Unfortunately they are particularly interested in a new software package recently launched and want to know how familiar you are with it.

Well, of course at the old company you would simply have asked the Training Officer to book you in and you'd be fully competent in the new techniques ...

Solution 1
Remember you need to keep your knowledge up to date to compete in the marketplace – especially if you operate in a fast-changing sector.

TIME MANAGEMENT LESSON 4
Build in training time to your programmes.

DIFFICULTY: Over-communication – too many letters and calls.

Have you noticed that now you're at home people seem to think you are free all day to chat on the phone – about nothing at all?
    And have you also noticed what a load of junk mail arrives through the door every day? It takes an age to go through it all – your secretary used to do it before so you never really noticed.

Solution
Over a day time exactly how long you spend on the phone – and differentiate between business and social calls. Do it again a

week later and a month later – see if there is any change in the amount of time or the balance between social and business related. For example:

Date	Time	Caller	Subject	Duration
2 Oct	9.26	Mum	Family	15 minutes
	10.35	Bank	Cheque	3 minutes
	11.08	Client	Meeting	5 minutes
	11.20	Son	Loan	13 minutes

If people know you are available they may give you a call for a chat – in which time you could have been talking to a customer or chasing some income.

And maybe you should consider stopping all the junk mail – but monitor it for a month because some of that junk may have a business lead hidden inside.

In any case, learn to be strict about how long you spend opening and reading through the mail – and do you have to interrupt an important report to look at the mail immediately and risk losing your concentration?

TIME MANAGEMENT LESSON 6
Limit your time on the phone.
Read only the essential mail.

ACTION PLAN FOR THE UP AND RUNNING PHASE

● Keep up to date with your marketplace all the time.
● Watch for opportunities to learn, speak and show your face.
● Keep your back-up admin and financial system in good order.

CHAPTER NINE

KEEPING IT GOING

Time Management Diary	
Check your cash-flow situation	Weekly
Keep an eye on the marketplace	Fortnightly
Keep in contact with your clients	Monthly
Make time for fun	Daily
Take time to sit back and think	Twice a week

SO now you have been going for a few months or even years and are doing pretty nicely, thank you – is there anything else to learn or will it all just continue to hum along?

Difficulty: One of the main reasons businesses close is poor cash flow – or the money not coming in at the right time to pay the bills.

This may stem from a number of causes, but one of the main ones is the owners themselves who are either too lazy, too inefficient or too shy to chase their cash.

Solution
Don't let this become one of those tasks you never get round to doing, just trusting the goodwill of your client to come up with the readies at the right time. Particularly in these difficult times, it is the small business, often the ones working from home, who

are at the end of the payment line and can lose out catastrophically.

TIME MANAGEMENT LESSON 1

When you've done the work satisfactorily make the time to control your outstanding credit. It could be life or death – and if you delay the first time, they will think it does not matter to you how slow they are.

DIFFICULTY: Business has been great; lots of projects completed, lots of products sold for a long time now and so far you perhaps haven't needed to go out and look for new contracts – they have come tumbling or at least sauntering into your lap at a good solid rate.

And anyway, you are very good at what you do, all your clients – well, you have only a few in number but they keep coming back – say they are pleased with your work. So why look to overload yourself and risk taking on too much and reducing the quality?

The next thing you know is that your best customer has gone bust and the other small contracts in your line are in a sector that somehow is going into decline. And here you are suffering from the feast-to-famine syndrome within a few weeks.

Solution
Never forget you are only as good as your last contract or sale. Customers disappear for many reasons, many of them entirely outside your control and you are left with an excellent reputation for good work but no work to show for it and several ongoing overhead expenses threatening in the near future.

You must always strike a careful balance between doing your current work and creating your next opportunity. Many people who are excellent performers fall into the trap of working now to the exclusion of developing for the future – they fill their time totally with actually carrying out the work and completely forget that they must have more of the work to do if they are going to continue in business.

TIME MANAGEMENT LESSON 2
Build business development time in to your ongoing plan.

DIFFICULTY: The Workaholic.

This is often a problem with new home-based workers that becomes a habit, then an addiction, eventually taking over the whole domestic environment.

When you first set up business from home, especially if it comes after redundancy or a career break and you feel very anxious about proving your ability to succeed, you feel, quite rightly, you must give it your very best and show total commitment to the targets you have set. This laudable approach does, however, tend to become over-exaggerated and you can take on the evangelical mask of the newly-converted. Everything, everybody and every minute of your waking life is taken up with work-related thoughts, activities and concerns.

This is all very well for the individual starting up and may lead to initial success – which only encourages you in the behaviour! But what about the other players in your domestic environment? Whatever happened to the quality of life philosophy you used to extol – the quality time you spent with your friends and family. You can lose your sense of proportion very quickly – both if you do very well at your business and if you have a slow start.

It is vital to remember the other parts of human existence and keep them in good condition at the same time as keeping the Bank Manager sweet.

Solution
Keep your work in perspective – you are a human being with emotional as well as financial needs.

Involve your friends and family in your overall plan and learn to lean on them – people love to help other people, it makes them feel good. Remember you will be a very boring companion if your only subject of conversation is your work – even if you do have the most fascinating area of knowledge, people can tire of it after a while.

And remember that your friends and family are also entitled to pursue their own interests and to receive attention from you.

After all, you probably leaned very heavily on their emotional, practical and possibly financial support when you were starting out.

Get things in proportion – you must decide whether your weekends are sacred or whether you don't take calls after 6 p.m. Do you really need to go to that meeting on Thursday evening or would your time be better spent in the overall scheme of things by watching television with your children or visiting your friend in hospital?

TIME MANAGEMENT LESSON 3

Build in fun and health time.

Build in holiday time – maybe not at the usual times you have always taken them but with a degree of flexibility to match peaks and troughs in your business.

DIFFICULTY: The distractions – all the things that get in the way of your work.

Have you ever noticed how, when you are just getting down to that difficult design at last, the phone rings? Or just how many callers turn up in a day? You never realized just what a social centre your own home was for the other members of your family and their friends. Or how guilty you can feel about not mowing the lawn while it's fine.

The list of potential obstacles to working effectively and consistently from home is endless – that is why recent retirees say they don't know how they ever found time to work because they are constantly occupied with tasks at home.

Solution
First you need to calculate the potential risks to your concentration and the relative merits of getting on with income generation as opposed to incurring the wrath of whoever because you haven't done the washing up.

This refers back to our original point – establishing your objectives. Remember that they frequently change and need to be reviewed. This may in turn mean that you need to reallocate your time – either on a temporary or a permanent basis to take account of changed circumstances. If someone is ill at home, it is obviously sensible to take advantage of your being home-based rather than getting your partner to stay away from his or her organization-based job.

TIME MANAGEMENT LESSON 4
Build in distraction time to your schedule – and add on an extra amount for unexpected intrusions.

DIFFICULTY: Not seeing the wood for the trees.

Another facet of the 'doing not developing' problem when you concentrate so hard on the present with its operational stresses, is that you completely fail to foresee future constraints on the horizon or even fail to see the disaster you are creating around you by not occasionally taking a step back.

Solution
You need to allocate both time and effort to making regular objective reviews of where you are going, what you have achieved and how you need to act to improve in the future. It may be more of the same or it might be a completely new direction but it takes considerable discipline of both thought and time to devote potential income-generating hours to blue-sky gazing.

TIME MANAGEMENT LESSON 5
Build in thinking time.

ACTION PLAN FOR KEEPING GOING PHASE

- Keep a check on your cash flow and chase it.
- Make sure you know where your next job is coming from.
- Plan to enjoy life as well as work.
- Get used to thinking long term.

Ten time controllers

Set yourself realistic annual income targets

Break your months down in to achievable goals

Note down weekly activities

Use a daily 'things to do' list and tick them off

Balance working on the current job and ensuring the next one

Remember the world outside work

Keep up to date in your field

Don't escape into non-essential action

Face up to the things you don't like doing
(they usually take longer than you think)

Leave time to take your cash to the bank

PART THREE

THE JUGGLE
AND THE STRUGGLE

S O far in this book we have looked at managing time in an office setting, and when working for yourself from home. But what about when you have three jobs – although only one of them is likely to be paid – in the office, as a home manager, and as a parent? And what about the rest of your life? Where does that fit in? In this section we are going to look now at how you can balance all the parts of your life so that you can be fully productive whatever you are doing – and be happy about it, too!

Although all of us need to be able to balance our lives, it is certainly true that women bear the brunt of managing home and family responsibilities. This is not to ignore the increase in men who are single parents or who are supportive partners but merely to acknowledge the reality of the current situation. This is for three main reasons:

- Most men earn more than their female partners so their energy has gone more into their work responsibilities leaving their female partners to manage the home responsibilities.
- Society still *expects* women to be responsible for home and family and tends to judge them on how well they do this, and indeed attributes mishaps to their faults in this area.
- Women *themselves* accept this responsibility, try to be superwomen, and feel permanently guilty when they fall short of their own impossible standards.

So one of the first things we need to do is to deal with the guilt trip which most working mothers feel. Once we have accepted that it is quite acceptable to be working at all, then we can look at how to balance it all.

CHAPTER TEN

THE GUILT TRIP

M ANY people happily combine the roles of home and work, knowing they are doing the right thing for their family and themselves. Others, in exactly the same situation, have difficulty combining the two roles. This is because they feel guilty about leaving their children in the care of others and about neglecting the home. What makes the problem worse is that a number of myths and legends have developed over the years which often reinforce feelings of guilt.

What are these myths?

THE MYTHS AND REALITY OF WORKING

Myth Women who stay at home are better mothers.
Reality Who says? Ask any woman who stays at home and she probably feels she could be a better mother. If you enjoy your work you're more fun to be with than someone who stays at home and resents it. And vice versa. It's all a matter of choice.

Myth Young children need their mothers at home.
Reality Young children need very good care – but that doesn't just need to come from mother alone. Children benefit from having a number of good relationships. As long as you are happy with your system of childcare, they will receive the care and security they need.

Myth   Mothers who work don't spend enough time with their children.

Reality   Mothers who are at home all day spend no more time playing with their children than women who go out to work. It's the quality of time spent with children that's important, rather than the quantity.

Myth   Children have problems when their mothers work.

Reality   All children have problems – don't blame it on the fact that you're working. The same problems would probably have arisen anyway.

Myth   Most women only work for the 'little luxuries'.

Reality   If you're struggling to bring up a family single-handed, if you're struggling to pay the mortgage, if you're struggling to give your children a 'better start' ... you know statements like this are worthless. They are often made by people who are secretly jealous of your ability to cope with work and home.

Myth   Colleagues think less of you as a working mother.

Reality   Working mothers are just as efficient, competent and reliable as other members of the workforce, often more so. Most of your colleagues won't care whether you're a mother or not – and those who make an issue of it probably aren't worth bothering with anyway.

Myth   Women who work don't look after their homes properly.

Reality   It's all a matter of degree. Your home may not be shining like a new pin at the end of every day. But does it really matter? Is anyone less happy because of it? It's all a question of priorities.

Now we've dispelled some of the myths about working parents, let's look at the positive side.

WHO WINS WHEN YOU WORK?

The answer is everybody ...

WINNER – YOUR PARTNER

If you have a partner, that person benefits in many ways, not just financially. Just as important is the benefit of living with someone who is fulfilled, competent and confident – if perhaps a bit tired in the evening!

WINNER – YOUR CHILDREN

Evidence suggests that children with working parents are well-adjusted, sociable, independent and flexible – in fact, all the qualities which will stand them in good stead as they mature. Also, your children will see both parents in positive roles – working and caring for them.

WINNER – YOUR EMPLOYER

The workforce needs people like you. You are mature with a variety of skills and qualities to bring to your place of work. You've made the commitment to combine home and work – a decision which has not been taken lightly. Your contribution is valued.

WINNER – YOUR FAMILY FINANCES

Your salary provides the family with greater peace of mind from financial worries.

WINNER – YOU

Working outside the home can create a sense of value and achievement. It can increase your level of confidence and sense of fulfilment. If you are happy working, this will carry over into your family life and everyone will benefit.

CHAPTER ELEVEN

CLOCK WATCHING

S O now that we feel good about working, let's look at how to manage the balance. Let's start by looking at what we actually spend our time on over a week, and then focus in on a typical day.

Does this sound like you:

'If only there were more hours in the day.'

'I haven't got time ...'

'I wish I was more organized.'

'I'll never get all this done.'

'Help!'

We'll be looking in a moment at setting priorities, but first let's examine what is actually happening. On page 91 is a wheel chart with seven wheels. Each wheel represents a day of the week. Record your activities each day by estimating how many hours you spend on each activity. You could do this by using a different colour to shade in each activity with a colour-coded key box or by using a letter to represent each activity. Do this periodically through the day or at the end of each day. Don't attempt to trust to memory by waiting until the end of the week to do it.

Here are some activities you might consider:

sleeping

travelling

paid work

voluntary activities

relatives

children

pets

housework/chores/home maintenance

Clock watching

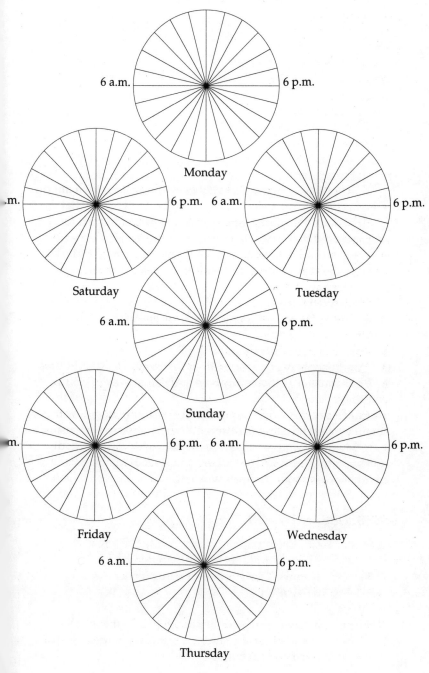

sport and fitness
health and beauty
hobbies
education/self-development
relaxation
religion
time spent alone
time spent with partner
time spent with friends

When you've done this exercise keep it handy – you'll need to refer to it later.

Now let's look at a typical day using Annette as an example (see page 93).

How does this day compare with one of yours? You'll probably find that a typical day in your life is taken up with many such routine activities. Even if you don't have children, many of the same chores, e.g. washing, cooking, ironing, still have to be done.

What often happens is that, like Annette, you get 'hooked' into a particular way of doing things for one of the following reasons:

● You've always done it that way.
● Other people expect you to do it that way.
● You've never really considered a different way of doing things.

It's often easier to look at someone else's situation and consider how they could do things differently than it is to examine our own. So what about Annette? Let's look at her day which she packs so much into and see where she is well organized and where there is room for improvement.

GOOD ORGANIZATION

6.45 a.m.	Got herself up and ready while the house was quiet – a little time and space for self!
7.30	Handed Christopher over to partner – good delegation!
1.00 p.m.	Made the most of her lunch hour – it could be argued that she should have taken a break instead of rushing around.

Annette's Typical Day

6.45 a.m.	Get up; have a bath; put on make-up.
7.15	Give partner a cup of tea in bed; wash and dress Christopher (aged one).
7.30	Hand Christopher over to partner; persuade Louise (aged 8) to get up and get dressed.
7.45	Make breakfast for children; wash up; feed cat.
8.00	Get self dressed; make sandwiches for Louise.
8.15	Leave home with the children.
8.25	Arrive at childminder's. Take Louise to school.
8.50	Arrive at work.
1.00 p.m.	Pay bill at gas board (remember electricity bill is sitting on kitchen table and curse); shop for evening meal; eat sandwiches.
5.00	Finish work; stop off to buy a birthday card for nephew; pick children up from childminder's.
5.30	Prepare children's tea.
6.00	Take Louise to Brownies while partner plays with Christopher, arrange with neighbour for Louise to be brought home.
6.30	Load washing machine; clean kitchen floor; wash tea dishes; tidy Louise's room.
7.00	Play with Christopher in bath.
7.30	Read to Christopher as he goes to sleep.
8.00	Prepare evening meal for self and partner.
8.30	Eat.
9.00	Iron (underwear and bedding); sort out bills; check bank statement; phone mother-in-law.
10.00	Phone call from friend who is having long-standing problems in a relationship – why doesn't she ask about ME sometimes?
10.30	Put out clothes for next day; set table for breakfast; write shopping list.
11.30	Bed – exhausted – no time for self. Where did the day go?

6.00 p.m.	Arranged for Louise to be brought home – good delegation again.
10.30	Prepared for the next day – assuming it was better to do it late at night, rather than the next day.

AREAS TO IMPROVE

7.15 a.m.	Gave her partner tea in bed – if they both got up at the same time, they could both have an extra 15 minutes in bed!
7.45	Fed cat – ask Louise to do it, she can earn her pocket money!
8.00	Made sandwiches for Louise – perhaps Louise could make her own – or eat school dinners.
1.00 p.m.	Forget to pay a bill – arrange to do this by standing order. Shopped for one evening meal – shop weekly, and in bulk.
9.00	Phoned mother-in-law – if this was a duty call, perhaps the duty wasn't Annette's!
10.30	Wrote a shopping list – use a photocopied 'master list', displayed on the fridge, to be ticked as things are needed.

It might be that Annette needs to delegate more of the household tasks – more about that in Chapter 12.

So now we know where our time goes – what can we do about it and do we really have a choice about how we spend it? Some people think that in order to manage home and work effectively the best solution is to work part-time. But does part-time mean more time?

THE PART-TIME MYTH

Many women returning to work after child caring choose part-time work because:

- 'I couldn't possibly care properly for the children *and* work full-time.'
- 'I'll have more time to fit in all the household tasks if I work part-time.'

- 'I won't need to rush around so much and I'll have more time in the evenings if I work part-time.'
- 'I'll feel less guilty working part-time and that will reduce my stress level.'

The problem is that it doesn't quite work like that. In theory we should have more hours at our disposal but all of the following things can conspire to give us no extra time at all:

- We actually work more hours in our paid job than we should because there is so much to do and we care about our work (many women in so called part-time work actually do a full-time job for part-time pay with no benefits).
- Relatives expect more time spent on and with them because we *only* work part-time.
- We spend lots of time ferrying children about whereas if we worked full-time we'd be organizing rotas and lifts.
- We are expected to be flexible and change our hours to suit employers' needs but this causes great childcare problems – at least if we worked full-time we could organize consistent childcare arrangements.
- It's more difficult to get partners and children to share in household duties because they think that we have more time to do these because we *only* work part-time.
- We feel guilty about using paid help – even if we can afford it – so we rush round on our 'day off' doing everything ourselves and ending up feeling just as tired and stressed as we would working full-time – and for less money!

Many women say that they felt no more guilty when working full-time than they did working part-time and they were able to be more organized. Whether you choose to work part-time or full time you need to be able to set some priorities for yourself around the non-work time at your disposal. Let's look at that now.

SETTING PRIORITIES

Go back to page 90 and look at the activities we gave you. Choose your top six priorities – those things which are the most important to you. Now look at your weekly wheels. Are the things that you are actually spending your time on the things that you have identified as being important? If so, great! If not, why not?

Quite often we allow people, places, and events to encroach on our time – without even realizing it. This happens for a number of reasons:

- Saying yes when you want to say no – worrying that people will think less of you if you refuse.
- Undervaluing time spent on yourself – because you see this as being selfish.
- Seeing people who you don't really want to spend time with – because you're afraid to upset them.
- Trying to do everything yourself and not asking for help – because you regard it as a sign of weakness.

The important point to remember is that how you spend your time is your decision. It's your time – spend it as you choose, on the things that matter most in your life. Have a look at your priority list from time to time – as a reminder of what *really* matters.

Now you know what you actually spend time on, and what you want to spend time on, let's look at a technique you can use to get rid of those irksome, time-consuming household tasks.

THE 3-D APPROACH TO JOBS

This approach is based on three principles:

- You have to spread the load of responsibility.
- You have to postpone doing certain things.
- You have to stop doing some things altogether.

When trying to bring your life into balance, there are three questions to ask yourself about household tasks:

- Does this task *need* to be done at all?
- Does this task have to be done *now*?
- Does this task have to be done by *me*?

Your answers to these questions will determine:

- Whether the task gets done at all.
- Whether the task gets done immediately.
- Whether the task gets done by someone else.

The following chart will help you to analyse your tasks.

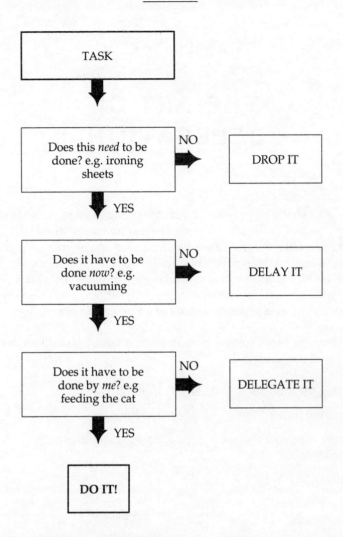

Of course, if the answer to all the questions is yes, then get on with it and do it, in the most efficient way possible. But you'll be pleasantly surprised how many things you don't need to do if you apply the three questions to each task. Of the three – drop, delay, delegate – the most difficult for many people is the last one. Some people, even the ones most skilled in delegating at work, have a mental block when it comes to delegating to partner, children, family, friends, and even machines. So the next chapter looks more closely at delegating at home.

CHAPTER TWELVE

THE ART OF DELEGATION

Y OU have already looked at delegating at work in the first part of this book. The term itself is frequently used to describe the process of handing over one of your own tasks to be done by somebody else. This doesn't mean passing over all the things you hate or find boring to whoever is least likely to object. It's about sharing responsibilities, because, as we keep saying, you haven't the time or energy to do everything yourself.

Here is a list of routine household and family tasks. Tick the ones that *you* usually do.

feeding the animals	☐	ironing	☐
preparing meals	☐	washing up	☐
putting dirty clothes in the basket	☐	doing the washing	☐
		setting the table	☐
emptying the bins	☐	dressing the children	☐
making children's sandwiches	☐	watering plants	☐
writing out the shopping list	☐	tidying the living room	☐
		cleaning windows	☐
picking up and putting away toys	☐	making beds	☐
putting shopping away	☐	shopping	☐
planning menus	☐		
cleaning the bathroom	☐		

The number of ticks you have will depend on:
- The number of people around to help you.
- The machines and other resources you use at home.
- The ages of your children.
- The attitudes of the people you live with about who should do those jobs.
- Your own attitude to delegating.

We need to look at your own attitude next.

DELEGATING – THE BARRIERS

Some reasons were given in the first part of this book for why people might be unwilling to delegate, but here we're going to concentrate on why you might not delegate at home.

Look at the ticks you made about the jobs you do and why you as opposed to anyone else does them. Do any of the following reasons apply to you?

I CAN DO THEM QUICKER MYSELF.

I'M TOO BUSY. IT WOULD TAKE ME TOO LONG TO EXPLAIN WHAT THEY HAVE TO DO.

I'M THE BEST ONE TO DO THEM.

That's right. You've had more practice. But if you spend a little time now teaching someone else how to do the task, you'll save yourself much more time in the long run.

IT'S TOO MUCH OF A HASSLE. THEY MIGHT DO THEM WRONG

They may make mistakes initially, but be patient. That's how we all learn – through making mistakes. You'll need to be on hand to show ways of making improvements but be confident in the ability of your 'delegates' to be as competent as you are in time.

IT'S MY RESPONSIBILITY AS MOTHER/WIFE/DAUGHTER

If you believe this then you are putting unfair pressure on yourself. Sure – the adverts and stories we see and read paint a vivid picture of how it is to be the perfect wife, mother or daughter. But you're unlikely to achieve perfection in even one of these roles, never mind them all – so don't even try.

I WANT TO KEEP CONTROL OF THESE TASKS

Ask yourself why. You may be causing yourself a lot of anxiety and problems by insisting on exerting control over all household tasks. You may also be increasing other people's expectations of what you should be doing – and making their lives a lot easier by doing it all yourself.

I MIGHT NOT BE AROUND IF THEY GET INTO DIFFICULTIES

Make sure you give adequate instructions (more about this shortly). You don't need to hang around. In fact, you may be seen as interfering if you do. If there are problems you'll find out about them. Make sure you tell the person how well they've done the task – we all need encouragement and showing appreciation is a good way to motivate them to continue!

I'M NOT SURE IF THEY'RE OLD ENOUGH/CAPABLE

You won't know what they can do until you give them a chance to prove themselves. They may surprise you!

THEY'LL OBJECT WHEN THEY SEE I'M OFFLOADING MY TASKS ONTO THEM

They may object. That's true. After all, they've expected you to do it up to now. Give them time to get used to the idea.

THEY MAY PROVE TO BE BETTER THAN I AM

Terrific!

I'LL GET THE BLAME IF THINGS GO WRONG

Not necessarily. It depends on how good your instructions were.
We'll come back to this in a moment.

TRYING TO DO EVERYTHING MAKES ME FEEL GOOD

And causes a lot of resentment in others. Ask yourself why you
enjoy feeling this way if it's true – and then look for ways of
feeling good without having to do everything.

I'VE ALWAYS DONE THEM/EVERYONE EXPECTS ME TO DO THEM

And you could well be the one to carry on, unless you revise
your own and other people's expectations of what you are
prepared to do. Your well-being is important, as is your time.
Just because you've always done something doesn't mean to say
you should have to continue. It won't necessarily be easy to
change the habits of a lifetime, but try starting to consider why it
should always be *you*.

THERE'S NOBODY ELSE TO DO THEM

There may be somebody you haven't initially thought of as
being capable or competent. More on who to delegate to later.

THESE TASKS DON'T REALLY TAKE A LOT OF TIME ...

Maybe one task doesn't. But add up all the time you spend
doing household tasks – look back at your wheel – that's how
much time you could gain by delegating.

DELEGATING SOUNDS LIKE NAGGING

It doesn't have to. Read on ...

So these are the barriers to delegating that we have to
remove. Perhaps it will help if we remind ourselves of the
payoffs of delegating.

DELEGATING – THE BENEFITS

You've already considered the payoffs of delegating at work. Here are some payoffs of delegating at home:

- You'll feel less stress and tiredness.
- You won't feel the same frustration at trying to do everything yourself.
- You won't resent having to do things for others who don't appreciate what you do.
- Your family will be pulling together like a team.
- You and your family can spend more time together.
- There will be less tension.
- Children will be encouraged to use their initiative.
- Children are more likely to become independent.
- Children, particularly younger ones, like to participate.
- Children learn that home and family jobs don't just belong to mum.
- You'll communicate better as a family.
- You'll have more time to spend on other things.

You may need to be convinced of the truth of some of these statements but don't know it until you've tried it! When you've got into the swing of delegating at home you'll probably be able to think of a few more. Now, what about the what and to whom of delegating?

DELEGATING – WHAT AND TO WHOM?

Here are some of the tasks you could delegate at home:

- Tasks that you are doing for others which they could – with a little instruction – be doing for themselves.
- Tasks which benefit the whole family.
- Tasks which require expertize that you don't have.
- Tasks which others may have more time or talent to perform.
- Tasks which are fiddly.
- Tasks which are time-consuming.

WHO TO DELEGATE TO?

Your partner
If you have a partner, this person is the obvious choice to
delegate to and, often, the most difficult. Basically, your partner
is capable of anything you are – it's choosing the moment to say
so! Choose your moment carefully. Explain how you feel. List
the benefits of your working. It may just do the trick!

Your children
Children usually relish extra responsibility – if you're careful
with your wording! Making their beds may be a chore to you,
but an exciting challenge to them (before the novelty wears off).
   When the novelty does wear off, blackmail may work! Pocket
money dependent on certain tasks being done each week usually
works as an added incentive. The other point about children is
that we often underestimate their abilities. Quite young children
can set the table, empty bins, dust, tidy toys and close drawers.
Older ones can wash up, care for pets, dress younger children,
cook simple meals and make you a cup of tea. Where children
are concerned, don't expect their standards to be as high as
yours. They're going through a learning process – and so are
you. Grit your teeth, and offer praise – they'll get it right in the
end.

Family and friends
Don't be afraid to use the services of other helpful people. It's
not so much delegating in this case as asking for help or
negotiating services. If your mother-in-law offers to make a cake
– let her. If your best friend offers to take the children
swimming, let her. There'll be other occasions when you can pay
these people back with some service of your own. Skill-
swapping is invaluable to a working parent.

Paid help
If you can afford it, use it. If you feel it's a luxury you can't
afford, try a little calculation. How long do you spend in
household chores each week? How better could you use that
time? How highly do you value that time? Does paid help still
seem a luxury? Remember, it's the *value* you place on your time
which is important. Not the time itself.

Machines
Which do you use currently? Which would you like? Kitchen appliances are not a luxury for working people – they are a necessity. Admittedly, none of them is cheap, but it's the same old story of valuing your time. If you find it easier to justify, work it out on a financial basis.

So how do you put these ideas into action?

THE TEN STEPS OF DELEGATING

1 Describe what you want to be done – room tidied, bin emptied, table laid, etc.
2 Explain how the job is to be done with step by step instructions.
3 Let the person know what standards you expect. How will they know you are satisfied?
4 Stop and wait for any questions that may be asked. You might assume they understand when they don't.
5 Ask if they understand. Check understanding and listen to what is said.
6 Let them know that *they* are responsible for completing the task successfully.
7 Give some examples to show what you mean. Demonstrate or describe.
8 Provide what is needed to complete the task. You can't expect a job to be done properly without the right resources to hand.
9 Set a deadline for completion.
10 Check the work and thank the person.

So – does it work in practice? Here's an example of a mother delegating the task of setting the table to her six-year-old son.
'Christopher, will you set the table for dinner please? I want you to put out four knives, forks and spoons. Also the salt and pepper and the sauce. Remember the forks go on the left and the knives go on the right – that's the side nearest the window. I'd like you to finish it in the next five minutes as that's when dinner will be ready. We'll all be ready to eat then so it's quite an important job I've asked you to do. Do you understand what I

want you to do? Now – you tell me what needs to go on the table ... Good ... The knives, forks and spoons are in the drawer, the salt and pepper are near the bread bin, and here's the sauce. Come and find me if you need help. As I said, dinner's in five minutes so I'll just check the plates are warm.'

Later – 'Right Christopher – let's see how you got on. That didn't take long did it? Everything is in the right place – well done. That's a really big help. I'd like this to be your special job from now on.'

Delegating tasks takes time – especially at first. But it *is* worth it in the long run and once people know exactly what to do you won't need to explain in so much detail in the future. Of course, the fact that you delegate properly doesn't mean that tasks will be done cheerfully or that it will be done exactly as you would do it. Doing things well takes practice and no one will ever do anything exactly the same as you so don't look for that either – and don't forget that important 'thank you' and 'well done' – it works wonders.

You might like to go back and look at some of the household jobs you do. When choosing which ones to delegate ask yourself the following questions:

● What would be the benefits to me of delegating this task?
● Who am I going to delegate to?
● When am I going to delegate it?
● What will I say using the ten steps?

Delegating is one way to make extra time for yourself. Now let's look at some other ways of finding time.

CHAPTER THIRTEEN

TRIED AND TESTED TIME TIPS

YOU may find that you are using some of these tips already – and you may have more of your own to add. Don't forget to pass on your tips to others – that's how I got some of these!

LEARN TO SAY NO

This is so important that we'll come back to it in a moment.

USE A 'TO DO TODAY' LIST

Most people find this list important. Do it last thing at night for the following day. Number the tasks and also put the time the task needs in an adjacent column. Looking at how long you need for each task helps you to define priorities. And remember – always put off until tomorrow what really doesn't have to be done today! It's amazing how many things can be dropped completely by following this maxim! Don't forget to keep to the time allowance you gave yourself. Don't overrun or you'll be back in trouble.

DON'T TRY TO BE PERFECT

If you're constantly aiming for perfection – you're setting yourself up for disappointment. Be prepared to make some compromises with your personal standards. There are only twenty-four hours in each day – whether you are princess or pauper you have the same number of hours. Don't try to be superwoman – she doesn't live in the real world.

PLAN MEALS

Planning meals in advance means you can get ingredients from the supermarket when you go to do a bulk shop instead of at the expensive corner shop at the last minute. Planning can also include who does the cooking. I have an eighteen-year-old and a thirteen-year-old who each cook twice a week. They decide what to cook, which days they'll cook, and it's up to them to make sure the ingredients go on the shopping list. Friday night is take-away night so it means that I never have to think about cooking during the week – bliss!

USE A MASTER SHOPPING LIST

Most people, certainly most women, know the things regularly bought at the supermarket. Why not do a master list and give everyone responsibility for completing one part of it? In our house there are five of us – the three girls check three cupboards each, I check the fridge, fresh fruit and veg, and my husband checks the freezer and household and wash items. We started this when my youngest was eight and at first she needed to use it all the time (the list says three tins of chopped tomatoes and we only have one, therefore we need to buy two ...) but now everyone knows what we need so the master list is hardly ever used. It means the list is done in five different handwritings but it does ensure ownership of your part – if there's no coffee because Louise forgot to put it on the list then she has to go and get some ...

LOOK FOR SHORTCUTS

Hang shirts up while wet or in a steamy bathroom – it saves ironing. Talking of ironing, don't iron socks and towels (apparently some people still do!) Fold sheets *before* putting them in the tumble drier – it does work. Buy clothes with easy care labels and avoid those which say 'Hand Wash Only' or 'Dry Clean'. Pay your teenager to iron for extra pocket money – but don't pay out for things which need re-doing! Have things delivered if you can to save collecting them. Invest in duvets next time you need bedding. Use bubblebath to stop a ring forming round the bath. Look for any way possible to save yourself that extra bit of time.

BUY IN BULK

A weekly or even monthly food shop will save time and money. You probably don't have enough hours in the day to hunt around for bargains. The time you gain by shopping in one place will be well worth the extra few pence you spend. As well as food, it's also useful to have a stock of other items you never have around when you need them. Tights, birthday cards, wrapping paper and stamps are some examples.

COOK IN BULK

This is one of those ideas that sounds great in theory, but who has the time? It doesn't mean cooking a week's meals all in one go – although some people do. It means cooking a double (even triple) quantity of a meal you have to prepare anyway. Freeze the rest and you have a ready-made meal for a later date.

USE LISTS

Planning aids are probably the most useful tools you have. We've already mentioned a master shopping list, but how about a wall calendar in the kitchen which can be used for family activities – football, dancing, visiting mum, days out. A new list we've just created is a meal planner headed with days, person cooking, meal planned, people eating, special notes. This is useful for the cooks as they need to know how many people to cook for – if you don't sign up you don't get a meal as I have found to my cost! It also means that if you want to bring a friend home to eat at the last minute that's fine but you get the friend's meal – don't expect the cook to. And if you run a taxi service for your children – and what parent doesn't – then make sure they enter dates, places and times on the social calendar so you can plan your time. The great thing about lists is that once something has been written down you can forget what it was you were trying to remember!

PUT EVERYTHING IN ITS PLACE

A place for everything and everything in its place – or so they say. In fact, it's quite true. If everyone knows where keys, money, credit cards and socks are kept – there's a good chance you'll get out of the house in the morning. You could then progress to dusters, polish and the hoover!

PREPARE THE NIGHT BEFORE

This can be anything from work clothes to packed lunches. You may hate it at the time, but it saves the rush in the morning. You have a greater chance of arriving at work looking calm and collected and without lumps of margarine under your fingernails! Better still get people to do their own packed lunches. We used to have a ritual on a Saturday morning where the children made loads of sandwiches and froze them in sets. Then each morning they just took a pack out of the freezer on their way out.

DELEGATE RESPONSIBILITY

We've looked at delegating tasks but why not delegate responsibility too? Why do parents have to remember that today the school photographer is coming, that they need to take wellies today for the nature trip and that they need a cheque for school dinners? Children can learn very early on that they are responsible for their own destiny – it's in their interests to get themselves organized. You don't do them any favours by doing all their thinking for them.

DISCOVER YOUR BEST TIME OF DAY

People are either larks or owls. Larks have most energy, enthusiasm and patience in the morning, owls in the evening. If you can work out which category you come under, you can use your best time most productively, for doing demanding or unpleasant tasks.

DON'T WASTE TIME WORRYING

Don't spend time feeling guilty or worrying about working. When you're balancing home and work, some of your old commitments will have to be sacrificed. So don't worry about saying *no* occasionally, a bit of dust around the house, serving up instant meals now and again. Don't spend time worrying which could be spent doing other things.

KEEP YOUR SENSE OF HUMOUR

It will see you through many a crisis. If you do feel like crying, then have a good howl. It's a good form of emotional release and far better than bottling it all up inside.

DON'T DO IT ALL YOURSELF

If you need help then ask for it – don't martyr yourself to prove a point. And look after yourself – if you don't then no one else will. We'll be looking at time for you in a moment.

One of our first time tips was to learn to say no. We'll look at that next.

SAYING NO

It's the end of a long day. You've been overloaded with work by a manager who gives you other people's tasks, as well as your own, because you are competent at your job. On your way home you meet a neighbour. You agree to do her a 'small favour' by looking after her children as well as your own at the weekend. You arrive home late and are greeted in the hall by your children who want to know if you can drive them round to a friend's house. Your daughter wants to know if she can borrow a scarf you haven't even worn yet. In the midst of all this your mother rings up and wants to chat about the awful day she's had. On his way out, your partner asks if you fancy going bowling at the weekend with some mutual friends. You hate bowling! An hour later, when you are just beginning to unwind, a friend rings to ask if she can 'call round for an hour' – just when you thought you had the evening free to yourself. Sounds familiar?

How many times do you find yourself saying yes when you really want to say no? Think back to the time that you agreed to do something which you were reluctant to do – not things you want to do or which you are happy to do to help someone out. We are talking about the things you do because you can't refuse. What often happens is that we are taken off guard sometimes by a request, we don't have time to consider it properly and we say yes because we don't like to offend. Consequently we feel:

- Resentful towards the other person for asking.
- Annoyed with ourselves for accepting.
- Frustrated at this misuse of our time.
  So why do we do it? There are several reasons:
- We believe it is selfish or uncaring to refuse.
- Other people expect us to agree.
- The person making the request will be angry or hurt if we refuse.
- We think it is impolite to refuse.
- We'd feel guilty if we said no.
- We wouldn't be liked if we refused.
  Let's look at some golden rules to help us to decide whether to say no.

THREE GOLDEN RULES

1 Your time is as valuable as everyone else's and this includes your partner, your children, your relatives and your friends.
2 You have the right to refuse some requests that are made of you – and the responsibility to accept the consequences.
3 When you say no you are refusing the request and not rejecting the person.

Learning to say no is a skill, which is good news because skills can be learned and improved with practice. Let's have a look at the steps involved.

HOW TO SAY NO WITHOUT FEELING GUILTY

Assess the request
Ask yourself 'Do I really want to do this?' The very fact that you have to ask yourself this question may indicate that you are not happy to accept. Pausing, even for a moment, will give you an opportunity to consider your response. Ask yourself:

- Is this a reasonable request?
- Is it a priority?
- Do I want to do it?
- What are the consequences of refusing?
- Can I accept the consequences?
  The next step is to ...

Ask for more information
You may well need more information before making up your

mind. If you ask questions, it shows the other person that you are not totally committed to agreeing.

Refuse the request
Make the refusal short yet courteous. The intention is not to offend the other person and presumably you want to maintain a good relationship with them. Say things like 'I would rather not ...' or 'I don't want to ...' or 'I am not willing to ...'. Don't say 'I can't because ...'. If you do, someone will solve that particular problem and you'll then be expected to do whatever it was you didn't want to do in the first place! If you wish to postpone the activity until a later date you could compromise by suggesting another arrangement. Alternatively, you may wish to assist the other person by suggesting what else they could do.

Be sincere
If you say sorry when you are not, it weakens your stand and encourages others to play on your guilt feelings. If you are genuinely sorry, apologize firmly yet politely. Don't give a long-winded explanation. Make it brief and to the point.

Watch your body language
Your face, voice and body movements should reinforce what you are saying:
- If you smile it contradicts and undermines what you are saying.
- If your voice is harsh or abrupt you may offend.
- If your voice is low and you look apologetic it may encourage the other person to persuade you.
- If you fidget or appear nervous it may seem that you don't really mean what you are saying.

Speak slowly and calmly, maintain eye contact, make your movements natural, and match your facial expression with your words. As with all new skills, you will have to practise before you are able to refuse requests and feel comfortable doing so. Here are some tips:
- Try it out first in a safe situation – not on your manager.
- Don't expect to get it right every time – go easy on yourself.
- Practise – aloud, on tape, with a friend.
  And don't forget the payoffs.

SAYING NO – THE PAYOFFS

- You won't feel the need to lie.
- You won't agree to an unwelcome request, then have to wriggle out of it.
- You are less likely to feel guilty.
- You will communicate better with people.
- You will be respected for your honesty – people can see through excuses.
- You will have more time for your main priorities.
- You will have more control over your life.

CHAPTER FOURTEEN

COPING WITH CRISES

S O now we have our lives sorted out and things are going to plan ... but does that happen? What if things never seem to go to plan? Can you plan for crises?
What do you do if:

- The car breaks down on the way to work?
- The kitchen is flooded when you get home?
- Your carer phones in ill at 8 a.m. on Monday morning?
- You forgot to defrost the evening meal and the cupboard is bare?
- A friend phones in tears as her husband has left her?

Certain crises can be avoided with good organization and forward planning. For example, if you have a back-up childcare system, the fact that your carer phones in ill shouldn't be too much of a problem. However, other crises are beyond our control – human error or mechanical breakdown for example. So what can you do to minimize the impact of a crisis?

HOW TO HANDLE A CRISIS

1 **Stay calm**
   This has a beneficial effect on yourself and others. Pause. Breathe deeply. Relax for a minute.
2 **Consider the situation carefully**
   Take stock of the situation. Consider what is the best course of action. Don't necessarily do the first thing that comes to mind.

3   **Advise others what is going on**
    Keep people informed. That way, they'll be more willing to
    help.
4   **Seek help, if necessary**
    You don't have to cope alone. You probably need support
    and advice, so don't be afraid to ask. Most people will
    understand and rally round in a crisis.
5   **Take action**
    Take whatever you judge the best course of action to be.
6   **Evaluate how well you coped**
    When it's all over, ask yourself if you took the right course of
    action. If not, what would have helped? What would you do
    next time? And finally, is there anything you can do to
    prevent a similar event happening in future? You may find
    that if you handle a crisis well, you get a greater sense of
    satisfaction than if the crisis had never happened in the first
    place. That's not to say you invite crises – your life is complex
    enough without that!
    You may sometimes feel that you are on a treadmill –
dashing between work and home, cooking and cleaning, tending
to your family's needs. It may seem to be all juggle and struggle
to have the fulfilment and satisfaction being a working parent
brings. But don't give up – it is worth it. The secret is to stay
positive – you can, if you think you can!
    Finally, what about time for yourself? How much time do
you spend looking after *you*? Try the quiz on the following page.

1 **Sleep**
   a You sleep well at night and wake up refreshed.
   b You go to bed late and rise early.
   c If you don't get enough sleep, you try to catch up later in the week.

2 **Exercise**
   a You intend to do something very soon.
   b You play a particular sport on a regular basis.
   c You exercise in the summer months – or when the weather is fine.

3 **Diet**
   a You grab a bite to eat when you can – usually standing up.
   b You eat well and don't worry about what you eat.
   c You are health-conscious and apply the same standards to your own diet as you do to your family's.

4 **Time to self**
   a You make time for yourself and your own interests/hobbies/friends.
   b You take time to relax – and feel guilty.
   c You have no time to yourself at present.

5 **Stress**
   a You enjoy being under pressure – it isn't a problem.
   b You know when it's affecting you and have techniques for controlling it.
   c You are constantly under stress and wish there was a solution.

6 **Rewards**
   a You feel guilty spending money on yourself.
   b You treat yourself occasionally.
   c You recognize how hard you work and like to reward yourself.

7 Friends
   a You often find yourself accepting invitations and agreeing
      to see people you don't really want to see.
   b Friends have become casualties of your present lifestyle.
   c You make an effort to see your friends regularly.

8 Attitudes
   a You don't believe that things can change.
   b You are determined to improve things in your life.
   c You may make some changes soon.

Now add up your score using the table below.

1	a = 3	5	a = 3
	b = 3		b = 3
	c = 1		c = 1
2	a = 1	6	a = 1
	b = 3		b = 2
	c = 2		c = 3
3	a = 1	7	a = 1
	b = 2		b = 2
	c = 3		c = 3
4	a = 3	8	a = 1
	b = 2		b = 3
	c = 1		c = 2

20 or more: You're very well looked after, well done!

11–19: You need a better balance, read on.

0–10: You deserve better than this, pamper yourself a
little!

CHAPTER FIFTEEN

TIME FOR YOURSELF

Y OUR time management *must* include time for yourself. We're going to look in a moment at two particular aspects – your support system and stress busters. But first, what about time for yourself?

When you completed your list of priorities in Chapter 11, how many of them applied to you? How highly did you prioritize your own health, education, sport, relaxation – or personal time and space? If items which related to 'self' appeared on the list – well done! You are part of the way towards creating a balance in your life.

If there were no items relating to 'self' on the list – why not? You *are* important. Your *needs* are important. *Time* and *space* for yourself are important. Neglecting your own needs and interests can have a damaging effect:

- You become tired and irritable.
- You feel stressed.
- You resent others for 'having a good time'.
- You may suffer from minor ailments such as head and back ache – these are the early warning system that something is wrong.

There's an old saying – *All work and no play makes Jill a dull girl* (well, something like that!). It's also very true! Everyone needs some time to themselves to enjoy their own interests, hobbies and pursuits. It's called 'The Happiness Factor' and everyone needs it.

You are not doing yourself or your family any favours by 'playing the martyr' and neglecting yourself. You don't? Let's find out!

Tick the things you enjoy doing and add any of your own to the bottom of the list.

118

Sport (watching)	☐	Gardening	☐
Sport (playing)	☐	Shopping	☐
Eating out	☐	Reading	☐
Keep fit	☐	DIY	☐
Cooking	☐	Theatre	☐
Cinema	☐	Studying	☐
Hobby	☐	Music	☐
Jacuzzi	☐	Relaxing	☐
A night of romance!	☐		

Hopefully, you'll have ticked at least three things that you are doing at present. If not, identify three things that you are going to do and decide when you are going to do them.

If you want to do something badly enough, you'll make the time. As we said earlier, you are the one who controls your time – you make the choices. If you make the time for one or more of your Happiness Factors, you'll benefit enormously. It doesn't have to be a day or even half a day – although that sounds like bliss. One hour, three times a week is fine. It'll help you recharge the batteries and increase your energy levels.

Here are some ideas from women managing the balance.

'I've written my Tuesday night evening class on the calendar in red felt-tip pen. The whole family knows that is MY time.'

'I now know why men find 'the potting shed' such a great relaxation!'

'I meet an old school friend for lunch once a month and it's a real boost.'

'I find the physical activity involved in badminton relieves all my stresses and strains.'

'Curling up with a good book and a glass of wine is my idea of heaven.'

'I get up an hour earlier three times a week so I can do my workout in peace and quiet.'

Apart from time to yourself, another good way of helping reduce your stresses and strains is to have a good support system.

A GOOD SUPPORTERS' CLUB

There's nothing like having someone to turn to when you need them.

- Someone to listen to your troubles.
- Someone to offer advice.
- Someone who understands your problems.
- Someone to go out with.
- Someone to laugh with.
- Someone to help you out in a crisis.
- Someone to look after the children in an emergency.
- Someone just like you.

And the 'someone' can be as many friends, family and colleagues as you wish. If you've never thought about this before, perhaps now is the time to do so. Spend a few minutes thinking about who can support you. The more names you can think of, the more support you get.

Finally, here are some ideas on how you can reduce those stresses and strains.

TEN STRESS BUSTERS

1 **Establish time for family fun**
Allocate at least one day a month for a family activity – a picnic, meal out, a day at the zoo – whatever the family enjoys. It gives everyone something to look forward to and means you spend time together.

2 **Spend some time alone**
If the idea of time alone appeals, then take yourself away from everyone and everything. Lock yourself in the potting shed if you think it will help.

3 **Do something silly**
If you have children, this isn't difficult – you probably spend quite a large part of your life doing silly things. Humour is a great leveller and it helps us get our lives into perspective.

4 **Relax**
Slow down – in whatever way suits you best – take a long,

warm bath, have a sauna, listen to music, practise yoga –
anything to help you unwind mentally and physically.

5 **Cut down on excesses**
The things we think help us, often have quite the opposite
effect. One gin and tonic to help you unwind is fine. But what
about the second and third? A good tip is to get someone else
to pour – they won't be quite so generous with the measures!
Alcohol is one example. The same applies to cigarettes,
caffeine, pills, even sweets and chocolates.

6 **Build relationships**
Not just inside your family – there's a big world out there. If
you can find the time, try getting involved with a church/
community group or helping out an elderly neighbour. It will
be a complete change of scene and will help you forget your
own problems.

7 **Try something new**
Anything from a new sport or hobby to that ambitious recipe
you saw in a magazine. Choose something which taxes you
mentally or physically. Something completely different from
the run-of-the-mill activities. Taxing activities will actually
help you unwind.

8 **Get a good night's sleep**
For some people this is six hours, for others it's nine.
Whatever you need – make sure you get it. If you have a
baby who wakes in the night this is clearly out of the
question, but for most people it's possible. Don't watch that
trashy American soap until midnight, don't start the ironing
at 11.30 p.m. Go to bed instead. You and everyone else will
feel the benefits the next day.

9 **Tackle problems head on**
If your stress is caused by a problem hanging over your
head like a black cloud, don't ignore it. It won't go away. In
fact the longer you leave it, the worse it seems to get. Once
you tackle it, it won't seem half as bad as you imagined it
would be.

10 **Spend time with someone special**
These are the people who really matter in your life – your top
priorities. Whether it's your partner, friend or children –
make time for them. Talk together, laugh together, be
together. They're the ones who make it seem all right.

TEN GOLDEN RULES FOR EVERY BUSY PERSON

Here are ten golden rules to finish off with. Write them out and pin them up somewhere – and look at them regularly!

1 I am not on call to all of the people all of the time.

2 I have needs of my own which may not be the same as my family's, my colleagues', or my friends'.

3 I don't have to say yes to every request that is made of me.

4 I don't have to carry on doing something just because I've always done it.

5 Time spent relaxing is time well spent.

6 There's no such thing as the 'perfect wife/husband', 'perfect parent', or 'perfect child'.

7 Time spent feeling guilty could be spent doing more enjoyable things.

8 I shouldn't always do it for them if they are capable of doing it for themselves.

9 I should give myself the same care and consideration that I give to others.

10 I should remember, at all times, especially in the face of criticism, difficulties and anxiety that ... *I am doing the best that I can!*

INDEX

The Ten Top Time-Wasters: the results of a survey conducted by the BBC and The Industrial Society, January 1993:

1 Telephone interruptions
2 Colleagues dropping by
3 Poor exchange of information between departments
4 Problems with computers
5 Changing priorities
6 Lack of corporate planning
7 Colleagues' poor listening skills
8 Poor company structure
9 Moving goal posts
10 Correcting errors

Also published by BBC Books:

How do you Manage? by John Nicholson
Business of Assertiveness by Rennie Fritchie
Give and Take by Jack Gratus
Managing Pressure by Paul Stamp & Helen Froggatt
Negotiating by Vanessa Helps
Speak for Yourself by John Campbell
Women and Power: How Far Can We Go? by Nancy Kline